NEW DIMENSIONS

Da Capo Press Series in
ARCHITECTURE AND DECORATIVE ART
General Editor: ADOLF K. PLACZEK
Avery Librarian, Columbia University

NEW
DIMENSIONS

THE DECORATIVE
ARTS OF TODAY IN
WORDS & PICTURES

by
PAUL T. FRANKL

DA CAPO PRESS • NEW YORK • 1975

Library of Congress Cataloging in Publication Data

Frankl, Paul Theodore, 1886-
   New dimensions.

   (Da Capo Press series in architecture and decorative
art)
   Reprint of the ed. published by Payson & Clarke, New
York.
   1. Art, Modern—20th century. 2. Decoration and
ornament. 3. Art industries and trade. 4. Interior
decoration. I. Title.
N6490.F7   1975   709′.04   75-15851
ISBN 0-306-70741-1

This Da Capo Press edition of *New Dimensions* is an unabridged repub-
lication of the first edition published in New York in 1928.

Copyright, 1928, by Payson and Clarke Ltd.

Published by Da Capo Press, Inc.
A Subsidiary of Plenum Publishing Corporation
227 West 17th Street, New York, N.Y. 10011

NEW DIMENSIONS

"Skyscraper Furniture," designed by P. T. Frankl.

NEW
DIMENSIONS

THE DECORATIVE
ARTS OF TODAY IN
WORDS & PICTURES

BY

PAUL T. FRANKL

PAYSON & CLARKE LTD
NEW YORK

To a Great American Architect and Creative Artist

FRANK LLOYD WRIGHT

My dear Frankl—

You ask me to write a foreword to your book. I suppose a "foreword" is some sort of introduction or preface.

A preface is either an apology or a sign of weakness somewhere, in any book.

An introduction is an unnecessary assumption or unwarranted meddling on the part of someone.

I've never felt otherwise about either.

Your book will speak for itself if you write with the authority and insight with which you are accustomed to speak.

No soldier like yourself, on the Fifth Avenue firing-line in the æsthetic crusade, with the experience of past years in that busy school-shop of yours could fail to say much that is pertinent, valuable and new in relation to that crusade.

Why should I vainly try to gild your own gold or paint your own lily.

I am eager as anyone to see your pictures and read your text, perfectly sure both will be a valuable contribution—out of experience—to the crusade, which I take it is in the cause of Style as against "Styles."

Faithfully yours,

FRANK LLOYD WRIGHT.

CONTENTS

ACKNOWLEDGMENTS

In compiling the pictures reproduced in this book the author has been generously assisted by his friends here and abroad. Special thanks are due to M. Albert Lévy, editor of *Art & Decoration, Revue Mensuelle D'Art Moderne,* Paris; Mlle. Thérèse Bonney, Paris; Herr F. Bruckmann, editor of *Dekorative Kunst,* Munich; and the *Architectural Record,* New York.

Many artists have also contributed and in each case their names are printed beneath the illustrations of their work. Every effort has been made to give full credit to the creative artist for his individual contribution and any omissions are due only to a lack of information.

Want of space and the physical impossibility of obtaining photographs has unfortunately excluded the work of many who rightly belong in these pages.

The photographs reproduced of the work of the author are printed with the permission of the Frankl Galleries.

LIST OF ILLUSTRATIONS

I. WHAT IS MODERN

MODERN is only a relative term. New things may be old-fashioned and they may be modern. But for that matter old things may often be considered very fresh.

How can this be? The answer is simple. Different times and different countries have their own ideals of beauty. The sense of beauty often repeats itself throughout the ages. The pyramids,—the ancient tombs of the Pharaohs—are extremely modern today in spirit.

There are cycles in art, and beauty of the past becomes alive and dynamic again as it again comes in harmony with the æsthetics of the moment. The pyramids were modern in 400 B.C.; but in the reign of Louis XV their angles were obsolete. But today again they seem near to us, more alive, more inspiring than the gilded quips and curls of the French period.

What is modern and what is not modern is mainly governed by our ideal of beauty. Let us try briefly to determine of what this ideal at the present day consists. In the human figure, which has always been the artistic source of inspiration, the slender, boyish forms are distinctly modern. If the Venus de Milo still holds her prize, which she no doubt won in a Grecian beauty contest, she does so perhaps only because she is a lady and is well deserving of courtesy. On her own merit, she stands today on very dangerous ground. She is far from modern. She represents more of the comfort of Greece than she does the speed of our age. She was once an ideal of beauty but today she is not our ideal.

The same ideal that inspires the artist in the human figure is also expressed in architecture and in almost every artistic endeavour of the day. Modern dress accentuates this aspect of the human body with plain, unbroken lines undisturbed by trimmings and unnecessary embellishments. In the same way, architecture itself endeavours to bring forward the constructive features of a building, and, by disregarding all additional decoration, achieves its effects through simple, rhythmic combinations of masses.

The creations in art that come nearest to expressing the ideal of beauty of their own time can be considered modern. Modern art has been created in all ages and among all people. Even the savages and uncivilized races have produced art very modern and full of life. Since the day when the pyramids were first built as symbols of power and monuments of a great Egyptian culture, whole civilizations have come up and declined. There were the empires of Greece and the empires of Rome and of Persia. The Golden Horde of Tartars swept across Asia and a good part of Europe, and Spain rose up through its power of navigation. Each empire has been doomed to decline—each civilization has passed away, but, in passing, has fortunately left us an intimate record of its own time. These records are written in art and they are not difficult to read. Through their art we can reconstruct the life of a whole people.

Art is the record of emotions. When art is made a thing alive the emotions within it cannot be killed or buried. Everything else perishes. Only art survives.

The history of the world could be written by making a careful record of the art of each country. Art has always expressed contemporary life—that is, art that is not imitation, and surely imitation is hardly art.

Each civilization informs its art with its own manner and character. In Egypt, the pomp and glory of the Pharaohs is reflected in almost every object handed down to us. In Greece, where many gods were worshipped, the great art was symbolized in the sculpture and architecture of the temples. During the Middle Ages, when God and Christianity became the sacred symbols of life, art was expressed in narrow, vertical lines pointing straight to Heaven and in what we now call the Gothic Churches built at that time. The life of the romantic period, a life of polished artificiality, is recorded in the architecture, furniture and costumes of the time. The record is complete. Each time has left its stamp in its art.

Creative art is alive. Art to be alive must leave off copying. It must be an expression of an artist's personality and that personality must be consistent with its age. It must be warm and glowing, must vibrate to be part of life. Copied art can neither glow nor vibrate. It remains rigid, and things rigid are things dead.

When a thing is creatively moulded it is flexible and alive. But you cannot take the finished mould and change it. A Chippendale chair cannot be altered into a modern piece of furniture. No period furniture could ever be made to look modern. The reason for this is simple. Period furniture expresses the life of the time in which it was created. We cannot live in those times, they are too far back. We must be content to live creatively in our own time.

Art of today must be created today. It must express the life about us. It must reflect the main characteristics and earmarks of our own complex civilization. Our age is one of invention, machinery, industry, science and commerce. The great complexity of things about us is quite worrying. Human nature cannot keep pace with modern invention. And, while complexity is a characteristic of our mechanical lives, it is the opposite of this that we seek for in æsthetic enjoyment.

The opposite of complexity is simplicity. The modern radio set, with its whole maze of wires, tubes and ingenious contrivances, is perfected in the laboratories of industry.

But as soon as it enters the home this entire complex mechanism is covered over with a simple and dignified cabinet. The simple lines of a modern steamer give little clue to the intricate machinery contained in the hull. Outwardly the modern automobile, with its dignified lines, is very simple compared to the curves and detail of an old coach. But beneath this simplicity a very complex machine is hidden.

Simple lines are modern. They are restful to the eye and dignified and tend to cover up the complexity of the machine age. If they do not completely do this, they at least divert our attention and allow us to feel ourselves master of the machine.

The final dress that we give to the things about us is usually very simple. This is true for architecture as well as for women's gowns. It is true for furniture as well as for the design of the new automobile and aeroplane.

Simplicity is modern. It is typical of our time. Our time is naturally the period in which we live, and it would be a little out of keeping to attempt to live today in an atmosphere of the past.

If we pause long enough to consider the matter, we soon realize what a dead and distant past a Louis XV room recalls to us. It has absolutely nothing in it that touches the life of today. We may want to enjoy this atmosphere of the past but our present-day selves cannot feel at home in it. It is difficult for us to be quite natural in a period setting. The setting is after all artificial and induces artificial manners. It asks for powdered wigs and lace collars and cuffs; and our trousers and long silken legs, in this setting, give us a vague sense of discomfort.

Recently a most definite change has taken place. This change was first prompted by necessity. The problem that has arisen is how to create a greater harmony between our outdoor life and the interiors of our homes. A great deal of experimenting has already been done in many fields, but the decorative arts have been slower in their development. The reason for this is because the home is a place that is still sacred and will not tolerate too many experiments or novelties.

While developments in decorative art have been slow, they have been steady and sure. More and more do we find ourselves out of harmony and completely out of sympathy with period and imitation antique furniture. More and more do we begin to hate walls covered with fancy plaster-work and ceilings that resemble giant wedding cakes. We are beginning to throw out the dingy hangings and scroll-work chandeliers, as well as the knick-knack cabinets and the gilt furnishings of past generations. Slowly but surely has this high pile of rubbish begun to disappear, to make place for newer, happier and simpler designs in colour and form.

What is modern in colour? In colour we try to express rhythm. The endless matching of harmonious shades of colour, as we did in olden days, was done for the sake of harmony. Today we try to express rhythm in the sharp modernistic effects which are characteristic of our time. This is accomplished by contrast. A colour contrast must be sharp and daring, but at the same time pleasing, in order to be modern. Through the study of Far-Eastern wood-blocks the Japanese colour tendencies came to us and were first recognized by the French impressionists of the nineteenth century. This began our new colour era. Ever since this time, flat colours have come more and more into use.

There is also the modern movement in furniture design which, as in all previous periods, is influenced by the architecture of its day. Architecture can be said directly to influence our furniture. But colour comes from the trend in fashions. At the same time ornament has been largely done away with and has been displaced by flat colours and all-over designs.

Modern furniture has several strong characteristics. It is built in flat surfaces and strong lines. The angles are decided and sharp. The proportions are well considered and the finish is beyond reproach. Sentimental mouldings and panelling are avoided as much as possible in order to gain the effect of extreme and severe simplicity.

In the main, it may be said that in the decoration of our present-day interiors the past is dead, for the things of the past are out of harmony with the life of today. We find ourselves out of sympathy with things that are so completely out of harmony. They worry us and make us unhappy, and there is no reason why they should be tolerated. The family album on the parlour table must give way to things less personal. The main character of things that are modern is simplicity—things have become almost impersonal and express little sentiment.

Public buildings have paved the way. The interiors of libraries, museums, and railroad stations, have developed a severe and impersonal artistic character. The last stronghold is now weakening and the modern home is bound to follow. More and more do people feel themselves out of sympathy with the ideals and expressions of the past generations and more and more are they discarding the records of old ages and sweeping clean in order to live in surroundings that are harmonious with their outward life. People are doing this because they find themselves happier and more at peace when their life indoors harmonizes with the life around them.

Simplicity is the keynote of modernism, but there are certain other characteristics that help to make a thing modern. These could be summed up as follows:—

continuity of line, (as we find in the stream-line body of a car or in the long unbroken lines in fashions;) *contrasts in colours* and sharp *contrasts in light and shadow* created through definite and angular mouldings and by broken planes. Things modern also have in them a definite rhythm such as we find in modern dancing and music and in the frank accentuating of form in fashions. They avoid imitation in material. They do not pretend to make wood resemble ivory but merely attempt to bring forward, in the best possible way, the natural beauty inherent in the material. They make a virtue of the material itself. Steel becomes steel. Copper is copper. Wood is wood. And paint is allowed to be paint and not made to resemble marble.

Informality is another characteristic of things that are modern, for it is also one of the earmarks of our present-day life. It is this trait, so characteristic of our time which has perhaps more than any other doomed not only the family album, but the fussy table on which it lay and the over decorated parlour in which that table stood.

What is modern? To be modern is to be consistent, it is to bring out an artistic harmony in our lives and necessary environments, a harmony between our civilization and our individual art impulses. What is our own art? Our own art is a creation that expresses ourselves and our time. It is an expression that is alive and while it acknowledges its debts to the arts of the past, it has no part in them.

II. RETROSPECTIVE—AND WHERE WE STAND TODAY

THE world that we live in seems very young and new. In our own time we have seen the growth of industry, the birth of machinery, and the triumph of science. We have witnessed at close range a revolution in the methods of war, government, industry, merchandising, engineering, medicine and law. The past recedes into a dim distance with so dazzling a present before us. These changes are closely bound up with our daily life. They represent the modern forces from which we cannot escape and are related to our daily activities.

It is not quite possible for a revolution to have taken place in music, painting, literature, architecture, science and politics, to say nothing of the industries, and leave the decorative arts untouched. It is not consistent or desirable that such a condition should exist. The decorative arts are as much a part of our present age as any of the other arts. The modern spirit, which is at present revolutionizing all the arts about us, has now broken through the last stronghold and has entered man's castle—his home.

The home has held out to the very end. It has resisted drastic changes. It is natural that this should be so for the home is the heart of our lives. It is a very private place, yet by its contents it reflects the individuality of the people who inhabit it. Its walls speak out and tell us who the dwellers are.

Yet it is within the walls of our home that we seek a safe retreat from the maddening crowd and from the nervous activities of our complex civilization. The home is closest to our birth and death, to love and sorrow, to dreams and happiness, and it is the last place to be risked with innovations and novelties. The experimenting must be done outside in ways that will not endanger or corrupt this heart of our life.

It is quite natural to fear the unknown and to maintain a dislike for things that we do not understand. With greater knowledge our dislikes vanish, and with greater understanding we gradually begin to accept what is going on about us. The startling new artistic forces that surround us can now be classified and analyzed. As soon as we are able to do this, we will lose all fear of the modern or the ultra-modern. There are today standards by which even modern art can be measured. A good deal of its direction, movement and growth may now be recorded.

If art is creative and a record of life, it, too, must move on. It is not possible in a modern world to have art remain in the state of the antique. Classical objects and antiques can be copied and imitated but they cannot reflect the life of today, and to copy and to imitate is hardly creative.

Art, to be vital and real, must be alive. And it can only be alive if it expresses in its own language the living forces about us. Creative works that are genuine are a reflection of their time and survive as a record of that period. And, more than this, they are the expression of the artist's personality. It is a method of transferring the product of his mind to the general public.

In the effort to become more natural and simple, the objects first to be discarded were those which were most frilly and carved with complicated designs. It is natural that the little bric-a-brac cabinets and the gilt furniture, upholstered with tassels, should have been the very first to disappear. There was very little controversy or stir made when they were removed. They seemed to vanish of their own accord and are very little missed by the present generation. They are hardly expressions of our time.

We have already brought out the fact that modern art is only a relative term and that the pyramids, while they expressed an ancient life, are today very modern in spirit. But we must also remember that art is an expression, as well as a record, of a civilization. In Egypt, art expressed the pomp and glory of the Pharaohs. In Greece, where they worshipped many gods, civilization was symbolized by the temple. In the Middle Ages, God and Christianity produced the marvelous churches, which we now call Gothic. In the same way, life in Russia expressed itself in its primitive religious paintings and peasant crafts. And life in the romantic French court, with all its artificiality, is recorded in the buildings, furniture, costumes and lacy textiles of the time.

On all sides we are hemmed in by modern forces. Compression has entered our lives in many forms. The modern automobile compresses the power of seventy or more horses in a motor as small as a lamb. The tabloid newspaper is the result of compression. Food is compressed into cans, drugs into tablets, and buildings are pressed together, and, for want of space, must shoot high into the air.

We have also brought forward the fact that simplicity seems a characteristic of our time. But this is only a surface kind of truth, for simplicity is a kind of cover for the complexity within us. It is true that our clothes and buildings and modern art are constructed on comparatively simple lines, with little ornamentation in detail, but it does not follow that, because of this, our lives have become simple. In fact, one is inclined to think quite the contrary and feel that life is more intricate and complex today than it ever was.

Invention, machinery, industry, science and commerce have all become more complex. We work under the pressure of time; we require speed to cover distance or to increase production. We need energy, and more energy, for tasks become greater and greater and enterprise urges us on.

Added to this pressure of time, we are beset by a horde of other forces.

Vast numbers of people are massed into great cities and centres of industry. Buildings are pressed together and must go up into the air to gain more space. Traffic must go underground for more avenues. Shops have become larger and more departmentalized in order to be able to distribute greater quantities of goods. Ships and trains have become more massive in order to take on greater traffic and gain speed. Machines have become enormous and are tuned up to their greatest capacity in order that they may perform the miracle of mass production. New problems have come before us, problems with which men were never faced before. These problems involve Speed, Mass, Traffic and Energy.

If modern art is an expression of our life, and if life is made up of these main problems, modern art must represent some of the forces with which we are surrounded. It cannot return to the antique and, at the same time, claim to be a part of our living selves. The new has sprung up so rapidly that, in many cases, the old has hardly had a chance to pass. A certain incongruity and discord is everywhere about us. The antique stands side by side with the modern. Old historic landmarks in our big cities are hemmed in and surrounded by towering modern structures. We look down into the chasm of Wall Street and still see the quaint silhouette of Trinity Church. The changes have been sharp and definite.

What has happened in architecture has happened also in costume design, painting, and all the other arts. The change has been forced by necessity and that necessity must have been very severe to make the change so radical. A good deal of experimenting has already been done in other fields that are related to the decorative arts. Painting and sculpture have both taken on new standards. And now the decorative arts have come to take the place they deserve. More and more do we find ourselves out of harmony and completely out of sympathy with the artistic productions of the past. The dingy hangings of the Victorian days, as well as the complicated chandeliers, are all destined to follow the path of the knick-knack cabinet and gilt furniture.

In all art movements of national scope, there are many factors that must be considered, and one very important factor is the material with which we work. Material is a natural product of the land. The fine marbles of Rome and Greece were quarried in those countries. The fine jades of Tibet are found in the rivers of that country. The clay, wood, metal, and other substances that the artist has to employ to make his creation must be part of his land. The Persians expressed their ideas in wool when they wove their marvelous rugs. The early Americans, who came to a primitive country filled with forests and strenuous conditions of life, expressed themselves with the wood that they found ready to hand.

But modern civilization has brought about a great diffusion of the world's substances. Raw materials are imported from many lands and brought to our very doors. And one of the great differences between modern art and ancient art is that modern art is not confined to the choice of several native materials. Perhaps a greater limitation would tend to simplify matters and produce better art, for it is in limitations that man can best show his genius. Of course, selection and discrimination are the main problems with which we are confronted. If to these factors we add elimination, we have the essence of modern decorating.

To put up something new in the place of something old is not the object of modern decorating. We do not have to replace the old because it is shabby with something that is entirely different. But we do feel that the old is outworn; not because of its shabbiness but because its aspect and character are not related to our lives. It is true that there is more amusement in the novelty of the new than there is in the conventionality of the old, but it is not only for the sake of amusement that the modern arts should be championed, for there are modern arts that are quite sober and extremely severe.

At the same time, the modern decorative arts are a good way behind developments in other fields and it is a debatable question whether these arts will ever catch up to the developments in the other fields. But there is really no reason why they should so long as they can conform and become harmonious with the life about us. There is no good reason why there should be a race between our inventions and industries and our arts. There should, however, be some sort of an understanding between these three Graces of our civilization so that their singing shall be done all in one key.

Both our industries and our arts have undergone great changes due to invention and machinery. There is a great difference between the handicraft of today and that of the peasant of old. The main difference between these two is a difference in character. One is quite personal while modern work is almost impersonal. The old is complicated and fully carved and embellished with design, while modern work is severe and simple and gains its effects from its flat planes, sharp contrasts, angles, light and shadow. These æsthetic differences are differences in form. Yet the spirit and the individual touch are the same in both.

Struggle produces necessity and this, in turn, spurs on the genius of invention. But art, on the other hand, is the product of a settled life, one that is quite peaceful and not worried. America, in the past, has been far too strenuous for a very definite settling down, and it is only recently that comforts and leisure have come to us. As a result of this we have a reaching out for artistic expression in all directions.

Great progress has already been made in most artistic fields. And now many creative forces have turned their attention to the decorative arts. Already certain inroads have been made, new ground has been broken and the foundation for a distinctive American art is already being laid. Let us see exactly what the changes are that have taken place, for now that the arts have entered the home their importance becomes quite vital. Let us also see what are the standards of measurement and how we are, from this seemingly impossible mass, to make any classification. In the chapters that follow we shall attempt a simple classification and discuss the practical sides of modern decoration.

III. BASIC PRINCIPLES IN MODERN DECORATION

THE room is the unit of decorating. Let us analyze this space by entering into a chamber. We are surrounded immediately by four walls. A solid floor is under our feet. Above is a ceiling. Our senses at once become alive. Not alone is the sense of sight stimulated with what we see before us, but other senses become alive. We can hear, smell, and, in a way, even taste the flavour of a room.

The sounds in a room are more important to its character than at first one would imagine. The sound of footsteps on a hard, polished floor is quite different from the soft, quiet shuffle of feet treading across heavy carpets. The sounds are characteristic of the different rooms. We may hear the restful crackling of burning wood in an open fireplace or the cool and peacefully monotonous beat of a small French clock. All sounds within four walls contribute to the character of the room.

In the same way there are delicate odours that spring from wall paper, calcimined walls, waxed wainscoting, linoleum, jute, fabrics, cedar closets, and special textiles that would tell us with our eyes closed exactly where we were. These odours, faint as they may be, influence the visitor. Creative effects must take factors of this kind into consideration.

In a way, it is also possible to feel a room. You can feel the cold of a marble floor or the warmth of a soft rug. You can also feel or gain a sense of rough plaster walls without even touching them. Soft, sheer side drapes and chiffon curtains produce a contrary effect, and the visitor would sense these things without requiring actually to touch them.

There are rooms that seem to have very definite flavours. These flavours spring mainly from the colours employed. Often the combination may be happy and the flavours agreeable, but just as often as not we are confronted with rooms which seem filled to the brim with conflict and war. This strife is immediately transferred to all our five senses. In this regard, a certain compounding occurs. What the eye sees the ear seems to hear. But added to our natural five senses is still what the Chinese call a sixth sense and that is a sense of understanding. And now the problem becomes more difficult, for most rooms that we enter attack this last sense. They defy all of our reason and all of our understanding.

It is through our senses that rooms transfer their atmosphere and character. There are rooms that spell quiet and rest and, on the other hand, there are rooms that seem quite conducive to working. In the same way there are serious and moody rooms and there are others which are gay and induce play. There are happy rooms and there are some in which nothing short of murder could fit the scene. These factors all spring from the interior atmosphere. The problem before us is to control the atmosphere and see how these effects can be managed.

Let us analyze briefly the main features of a room. In the first place, there are two parts;—the stationary part and the movable. Walls, floor and ceiling naturally form the stationary section, while furniture, hangings, draperies and all other objects form the movable.

The stationary feature of a room is the frame or hollow skeleton in which we are required to work. This frame is perforated or pierced with openings which we call doors and windows. It is within this perforated frame that we are required to express personality, atmosphere and comfort.

Our ceiling above should be plain and as simple as possible. The days for plaster scroll work and painted angels is passed. It should not catch the light in a glaring manner nor should it in any way call attention to itself, for, by so doing, it would draw the eyes and head of a visitor upwards and bring about an unnatural position. The tone and colour of the ceiling should be similar to that of the walls but perhaps a few shades lighter. The reason for this is quite plain. If the ceiling were darker than the walls, it would appear to hang heavy above and give the effect of being lower than it is in reality. At the same time, low ceilings are not to be condemned, for low ceilings often give great charm and intimacy to a room. The distinguishing character and charm of an early American room is the very low ceiling. This induces not only intimacy but friendliness and hospitality.

High ceilings are characteristic of mansions, palaces and very formal architecture. They are quite necessary for railway stations, libraries, schools and other public buildings. But their place in the home is very limited and it is difficult to explain why many decorators still insist on the formal and cold high ceiling. The effect of the height of a ceiling is easily controlled. A dark ceiling makes the room look low and a very light or white ceiling gives it the appearance of height.

All decorations, such as plaster work and elaborate chandeliers, should be omitted from the ceiling. Plain centre lamps are sometimes called for but the present tendency is to leave them off as much as possible. Lights are being made movable and concealed at the present time, as we shall explain in another chapter. Ceilings of different levels in the same house lend a great deal of charm and variation of atmosphere.

In the past few years, many changes have taken place in the treatment of walls and ceilings. But our floors have remained very much in the old conventional golden age of golden oak. Golden oak remains, and, strange but true, specifications for most buildings today call for light oak floors as though it were a thing quite desirable and unquestionably correct. Varnished light oak furniture has long been discarded but the light oak varnished floors which have all the objections that the furniture had are still tolerated. But, should we do away with the varnished oak floor, what could we bring into its place?

The modern floor, regardless of its material, must be as plain and as noiseless as possible. It is very much as Henry Ford is reported to have said once regarding the colour of his cars—"You may have them any colour you desire as long as it is black." Black is the best colour for floors, though scientifically neither black nor white could strictly be called colours at all. In certain cases, black may appear a little extreme and could with advantage be compromised to a dark brown. Black used in this way should not be considered as creating a morbid effect for it serves only as a background for a picture which should be colourful. It is because of the absence of colour from black that objects and hangings in colour when used against it as a background show off to their very best advantage.

Floors may also be treated with carpets. This requires very careful handling as well as a few words of warning. In the first place, Oriental rugs for floor coverings are very much against any modern spirit. There is little excuse for the use of Oriental rugs except that one has them around and one has grown up with the impression that they are of immense value and therefore must be held quite sacred. Some people are either born with or inherit a flock of Oriental rugs; others marry into a family of them. There are some, however, who set out deliberately to buy them and for such there is little hope or excuse. The illusion that rugs are of great value can easily be shattered by attempting to dispose of them. It is then very often that their intrinsic worth will sink almost as low as their artistic value.

The Oriental rug had a place for itself at one time when the Turkish den was a feature of our old homes. This den usually was decorated with lamps, old swords—usually imitation—Arabian flint-locks, saddle-bag pillows, brass battle-axes and gaudy gilt braid. They have all vanished into a faint memory but the rug is left behind as a symbol of a civilization and culture far removed from our own.

The decorative and cultural value of fine antique Oriental carpets that were woven by masters before the day when aniline dyes were imported into Asia Minor should not be slighted. These rare specimens and records of a past civilization belong on the walls of our museums and should not be exposed to daily tread and wear as floor coverings. Modernistic rugs in floral or geometrical patterns present the same objections as do the Oriental floor coverings. Designs on the floor are disturbing and should, therefore, be avoided as much as possible.

The ideal foundation upon which a room may be built is plain carpetings in grays, taupes, quiet browns or black. Any of these would give a solid foundation and provide a natural and simple background for a modern scheme. These carpets should have no borders which are darker or lighter in tone, for a border gives the appearance of a step and catches the eye as one is crossing the room. A plain solid covering would form the basis of a scheme, and allow for changes in decorations that time and necessity might require. And both time and necessity usually do require changes.

Returning to the walls of our room, it is here that a good deal more variety in treatment may be allowed. Doors and windows break up and cut into our walls. Of these we shall have occasion to speak later. But for the hard, flat surfaces themselves there are many variations of treatment that present themselves. Walls may be painted, papered, panelled or wainscoted; they may be covered with fabrics or finished in rough plaster. We may have combinations of any of these and there are variations of treatment each can present.

The simplest kind of treatment, of course, is to paint the walls. In this, the main consideration would be the colour. This colour must be related to the colour of the hangings that are to form a part of the room, and, because of this, it is advisable first to select the materials for these hangings. It is much easier to mix a colour from a cloth sample than to try to find a fabric to match or harmonize with the colour on the wall. A sample of the fabric may be brought into the room where it is to hang finally and here the paint may be matched. While it would be simple to bring a small sample of your painted wall into the shop and match your fabrics to it, still there are several objections. The first is that it is hard to find fabrics to match a given shade and colour, and, second, the fabric will never look the same in the shop as it will look beside the windows of the room in which it is to be used.

There is also variation in choice in the process of applying the paint to the walls. Walls may be painted flat, stippled or glazed. Panels made of strips of moulding should be used sparingly, if at all, and only after a careful consideration of the furnishings that are finally to be assembled in the room. Wall panels tend to create a series of frames in which it is often difficult to compose the picture with the furniture at hand. At the same time they make for a formality in background and this formality is only justified when it is strictly in harmony with the contents of the room. In other words, the furniture and objects must ever be borne in mind and it is only when these have the

28

character of strict formality that panelled walls are ever justified. There are also advantages in the flat, the stippled and the glazed painted surfaces. Each has its place and each should be studied for its effect.

Wall-papers have several disadvantages. In the first place, they are not over-sanitary and often retain a papery and musty odour, which is hard, and sometimes impossible, to eradicate. Besides these practical considerations, they often tend to create a surface that is not in keeping with the solid and flat character of the walls.

At the same time, wall-papers often present distinct advantages and their use may prove very valuable in places where decided effects are required. Their comparative cost is small and in the face of this we can often forget their failings, especially when we discover such charming and happy patterns as are found in many modern papers of original and quaint design. The objections, however, return to our notice when the novelty of a design wears off. In time, we usually weary of the pattern but then, of course, the expense of repapering is not very great. New papers in the modern spirit are now being manufactured both here and abroad. It is possible to secure machine motifs and even futuristic and cubistic effects as extreme as one chooses. There are modern papers in soft pastel shades that make for quiet backgrounds and there are papers, some of which are illustrated in this book, that present startling effects in contrasts.

Rough plaster walls have come forward in the modern scheme of decoration and their great value lies in the surface texture that is produced. It is the surface texture that is important. This texture often creates a harmonious character with many modern settings. It has one great and distinct advantage. It allows for an interplay of light and shadow and this is a characteristic of which we do not easily tire. While we often weary of a particular design or a special colour, a wall that has a broken-up surface and casts spongy shadows of varying intensity at different times of the day is not one that tires us readily. It provides a permanent background, one that is not easily destroyed or soiled.

Walls that are wainscoted tend to give a room a very formal appearance. If formality is desired, wainscoting is in order. But if wainscoting is called for it should be extended very high, as high as the picture moulding. There should be no half-and-half combinations. Mouldings used in wainscoting should be sharp and direct and not rounded in sentimental curves convex and concave. The great charm produced by wainscoted walls is a charm that lies in the natural beauty of the wood. Wood is a thing that is alive and the life in the wood should be preserved as much as possible. Therefore, very little finish should be applied to wainscoting. The natural beauty expressed

29

in the texture and grain of the wood is best emphasized when the wood is given large spaces and plain surfaces that are little broken up by mouldings and panels. These plain surfaces should not be painted over or killed with fillers and varnishes. They may be treated, tinted or waxed, but whatever is done to them great care should be taken that the life, which is the natural beauty of the wood, is not destroyed.

Still one more wall treatment presents itself, and that is the use of fabrics. When this type of decoration is called for, the fabric should be hung from a rather high picture moulding, very much as a curtain is hung, and it should extend to the very floor. A slight gathering at the top will create long unbroken lines and bring out the soft shadows cast by the folds. This effect of quietness and charm is in keeping for backgrounds and is very much the vogue of today. If the material were stretched taut across the wall this grace would be entirely lost. A simple heading at the top and heavy weights strung in the bottom will add character to this type of background. A room completely hung with fabric makes for slight formality but, surprising as it may seem, it creates an effect of space and distance. Walls covered in this way make a room look really larger than it is. The reason for this is that we imagine the hanging before us to be a curtain and we feel that there is always space beyond the curtain.

We have now completed the background of our room. In this we have done our best to avoid, except in the case of certain types of wall-paper, bright colours or definite designs. Walls are like the setting on the stage in which the play is to take place. A setting too elaborate and too striking in colour and design would immediately take the attention away from the actors and the lines in the play. Our colour, design and individual touches, which all belong to the movable section of the room, are the actors in the play. Here artistry and daring must be displayed. Here timidity is an enemy.

The reason many of our American homes look so pale and washed-out is because great restraint and caution was not only applied to the background but also to the furniture, coverings and other movable parts of the room. We have recommended a quiet and cautious background because there is a picture to be painted against this background. Restraint can be shown in the one, but if it be shown equally in both then the entire result will have a washed-out appearance.

The picture must stand forward. It must be interesting. And it must accomplish what it sets out to do. This picture is made up mainly of the movable features of the room. Let us bear in mind a single maxim which in a general way gives us a good rule to follow: restraint for the background and courage and daring for the movable features.

IV. DECORATIVE FABRICS AND THEIR USES

IN the previous chapter we divided our room into two sections, the stationary and the movable parts. We spoke about the main principles that govern the stationary features of our room and we reached the conclusion that individuality, artistry and daring belong to the movable features and it is in these parts that colour can be best expressed.

Let us pretend for a moment that we are to decorate a room. The first step, and by far the best and safest way to proceed, is to begin with the selection of our fabrics. We have already seen why it is simpler and safer to paint or decorate our walls after we have samples of our hangings. And this principle is not only true for walls but it is also true for the general scheme of things. We begin with our fabrics. We assume, of course, that we are free to select whatever colour scheme pleases our heart's desire, but the heart is not the only emotion to be catered to. We must have an eye toward the practical and also toward suitability. The gorgeous fantasies that we may build up in our mind's eye are sometimes not very suitable for the living-room that we are faced with, and would, indeed, be more suitable for a spare room in the country or perhaps a small card room in a large apartment.

The first step is the selection of the fabrics. In this we are free to choose any colour scheme that fits in with our plan, provided we have not already been tied down by Oriental rugs. To visualize colour, texture and design in masses takes long experience. This is perhaps one of the most difficult of all decorating accomplishments and can be developed only by much practice. Daily contact with fabrics and a careful analysis of each reaction toward each fabric will soon make one expert. A kind of fabric sensitiveness is quickly developed by daily discipline and study of the fabrics about one. When you see a new type of stuff or a material of new design, you should carefully compare it in your mind with other fabrics that are related or woven in contrast.

Let us take an example to illustrate the point. Supposing we are riding in a Pullman car. We look about us. Here we find the seats are usually covered with a kind of mohair velvet that is sun-proof and guaranteed to wear like iron, but the more we look at the texture and colour of this material the more we feel certain that our artistic senses are not much inspired. Therefore, we should at once be led to conclude that their use is restricted and, while appropriate to the Pullman car we are riding in and to other Pullman cars, the material is not one that we can safely carry into the home.

At the same time, the chintz pattern that perhaps pleased us in our friend's home would no doubt produce the same pleasure if it were used in our home. Likes and dislikes are very important factors and, while we may not have logical reasons for our liking or disliking of a particular stuff, our likes and dislikes should be considered seriously, reason or no reason. Sometime ago we may have seen a wall-paper in a certain hotel room which we have grown to dislike for apparently no reason at all. Once more we see the same patterned paper presented before us for a possible decorative scheme. Reason might tell us that it is a practical possibility but our emotional sense, the same sense which has originally started the dislike, prompts us to reject it. Our dislike has served us for a valuable guide and, in the same way, our likes can serve us and indicate what particular designs and colours will make us most happy.

While likes and dislikes serve us as our main guide, they should not entirely do away with reason and knowledge. An acquaintanceship and familiarity with the medium is most important. For this a practical judgment and a decorative sensitiveness are quite necessary. This judgment and sensitiveness should be brought into play, together with our artistic faculties, in order that we may clearly analyze what we see before us and profit from our experiences.

In working with fabrics there are several practical suggestions that may prove valuable to the decorator new in the field. In experimenting or trying out different fabrics to see how they look in different situations, it is best to avoid small cuttings and to use large sample lengths. Even these large sample lengths are often deceptive for they do not show the bulk relationship between the plain colours, or flat surfaces of the room, and the figured material. In working with figured materials, they should, of course, be examined in proportions large enough for the material to take its proper relative place beside the plain background. Unfortunately this method is not always possible, but an attempt should be made to see the fabric in its entire bulk. For this reason alone, the methods usually employed in schools, where students are required to work out their decorative schemes by means of small bits of fabrics pasted into scrap books, are misleading and of little value.

Design, colour and texture are our main considerations in the selection of fabrics. It must be remembered that a room can contain only a certain amount of colour and a certain amount of design. It is like a glass bottle that can hold its full quart of liquid but no more. Its capacity is limited and these limitations must be recognized. And within these limitations we must work.

As a rule we should be warned against using more than one type of design very prominently in the same room. Any designs that are eligible for the decorating scheme should be considered more than once. A great many of the best modern effects are achieved with no design at all and merely by combining plain colours in attractive and original ways. It is difficult to say at any moment what is a good colour or what is a good design, for a colour is only good in relation to what is next to it and around it; and a design is only good if its character fits suitably into the completed room.

In the selection of colour and design, it would be well to remember that fashions have moulded taste and have been the dominant influence for the decorator and designer of the fabrics. Simplicity, the guiding factor of our fashions of today, is also the keynote for our hangings and fabrics. Curtain and furniture trimmings, such as fringes, tasselled edges, interlinings, etc., all belong to the past. Long folds and unbroken lines accentuating the individual beauty of the material used, are in keeping with the simplicity of today's fashions and tend to make modern schemes.

Decorating is mainly a process of eliminating. Nowhere can this process of eliminating be practiced more successfully than in the upholsterer's art. Very few curtains, if any, really call for an interlining, for the day when curtains were designed to keep out drafts is long past. Efficient weather strips and more evenly heated rooms have done away with this necessity. For this reason, it would be a great mistake to continue the conventional practice of lining all curtains with cream-coloured sateen. Of all the materials used for linings, sateen surely is the least artistic. Fringes, corded curtain loops and elaborate Bouillon tassels should also be avoided, except in very special cases where peculiar conditions may call for them. These trimmings have long been the stock-in-trade of all upholsterers and there is still a good deal of stock to be disposed of. But their place is hardly with modern furniture, and it does not look very likely that they ever will return to favour.

Soft tassels with long silk fringes that are Chinese in effect but not in origin, like those used on evening wraps, may give a smart accent to a decorative scheme if used very sparingly. But all other types of tassels are quite taboo. We want our materials effective; we want our taffetas crisp, our satins oily in appearance, and we want our chintzes quaint and colourful. But velvets?—velvets I think we do not want at all. If linings are to be used, they should be made of attractive sun-fast material with an edge or slight fold showing as curtain trimming. The colour of the lining should either contrast decidedly or match the material of the curtain.

As a rule, curtains should hang to the very floor, unless there are good reasons to prevent them from doing so. A long line in the light of the window gives the room greater importance and accentuates the beauty of the material. The valances used to cover curtain rods and hide the window blinds may now be replaced successfully with a simple cornice board. This has the advantage of holding no dust and gives a plain architectural finish to the top of the window. Casement curtains should hang well below the sill. The reason for this is that light from the windows makes an unsightly line at the bottom of the curtains if the material does not come down to the very sill. Chiffons may be used to very good advantage when made up for casement curtains, as their transparency not only softens the light filtering through but also lends a pleasing effect of distance.

In the selection of colours for our room, great attention and a good deal of courage should be shown. In this, courage is most important for it is not sufficient to keep on matching tones of related colour to produce soft harmonies. It is often more important to get a good sharp contrast than a perfect match. Our great painters are not famous for their monochromes but for their daring accents.

Sweet harmonies of anæmic colours should not be our aim in decoration, but, on the other hand, neither should it be to produce jazz symphonies.

The palette of the decorator is quite different from the painter's palette. The painter may form new colours and shades of colours by the simple process of mixing, while the decorator must combine set colors with existing textiles and surfaces in order to produce his harmonies or contrasts. From the decorator's point of view, each colour has its own range and this range depends mainly upon the colours that he is able to add to a given colour. It would be well to consider what these different ranges are.

Of all colours, white has the smallest range, although scientifically neither black nor white can be regarded as colours at all. But for practical purposes we must call white as well as black a colour. White has the smallest range. And the reason for this is that, if any other colour should be placed beside it, it would at once change the appearance of the white to some faint tint related to the colour beside it.

Black and green have the widest range and combine with more colours, from the decorator's point of view, than any other members of the spectrum. Here is a list of colours that make a good match, or, as the French say, marry well:

White	*Red*	*Orange*	*Yellow*	*Green*
no colours	white	white	white	white
	yellow	red	brown	yellow
	brown	brown		red
	orange	yellow		blue
				brown
				black

Blue	*Purple*	*Gray*	*Black*
white	white	all	all colours
black	red	colours	but not
	blue	including	white
	black	white	

The art of decorating is not alone limited to the matching of colours but concerns itself also with bringing out colour values through contrast. The art of contrast is one of the secrets of good decorating. The decorators of the old school have avoided decided contrasts and unsentimental combinations. But the modern decorator, like the modern dress designer, has proved that sharp notes and impersonal touches fit in well with the modern tendency. A sharp colour contrast is not unlike a clearcut and bold design and both should be considered together.

The greatest colour contrast we have is naturally between black and white. One of the reasons for the modern preference for black and white, as well as combinations of gray and silver, is the fact that these colours are neutral and lend themselves to combinations with other colours. This is a great advantage in decorating and by clever handling can be made into a scheme quite by itself. But black and white decorations should not become a formula for all modern art. Black should not be considered as morbid or funereal in effect, for, when used as a background, as in a carpet or couch cover, it shows off well the brilliancy of all other colours placed against it. This effect is a happy one and far from morbid. Black brings out the full richness of all other colours used with it. Black can also be used very freely as a contrasting colour with green, red, blue, and, in small doses, with orange and yellow.

Of course, theoretically black is black and there is no difference between one black and another. But practically one could say that there are different shades of black. Jet-black has a bluish effect and Chinese black has a brownish cast. Black lacquer has a strong metallic sheen that reflects high lights, while black crepe absorbs the light as blotting paper absorbs ink and gives a dull, wooden effect. Each type of black has its own special advantages. Each produces an effect of its own and each should be studied carefully before it is employed in a decorative scheme.

White has a multitude of shades that are all very closely related and differ mainly through the texture of the surface. A white bear-skin on a white marble floor illustrates a contrast in the difference of texture. White is strongly influenced by other colours that are placed beside it and this should always be remembered when using white in planning an interior.

Gray and silver are closely related to black and white and can be effectively used together without the addition of another colour. The effect is cold and impersonal but, with proper handling, can be made to look extremely modern. Silver is used very much today in decorating, taking the place of gold. Even in the jewelers' art of today gold is being rapidly replaced by platinum and a white gold that resembles platinum. Mirror frames in silver seem to harmonize better with the glass in the mirror than a gold frame would and silver picture frames for paintings on the wall seem to give a pleasing and cool effect to both the picture and the wall. Our chief tendency in colour today is to get away from warm colours, such as red and brown, and to prefer cool colours and cool effects.

There are two main members in the family of cool colours,—green and blue. Green and blue are in direct contrast to orange and red, the important members of the warm colour family. Blue and green are very closely related and there are many colours that are so much on the line as to cause confusion. The Japanese make no distinction between one or the other and have but a single word to express both blue and green. Within the range of these colours harmonies are rather simple for we find that most shades of green harmonize with each other and most shades of blue also harmonize.

Cool colours make for distance. A room decorated in red will look quite small compared to the same room decorated in green. This feeling of greater space is made only by the employment of cool colours. A red carpet would also make the same room look smaller, while a green carpet would seem to give the same room more space.

Colours should not only be regarded from the point of view of matching and contrasting, as well as their effect of cold or warmth, but they should also be regarded from their intensity. If we were to paint a room in soft pastel shades we should avoid everything but pastel shades. This does not at all mean that the entire room must be sweet and without character. On the contrary it does mean that very decided contrasts can be achieved in these colours alone but the colour values must be kept equal in intensity. The paintings of Marie Laurencin illustrate this point very clearly.

Colour intensity is best used in producing very stagey effects. These effects are painted best with strong poster colours. But the decorator is not confined to these two types of colour handling. Chinese effects may be sometimes taken from the very fragrant colours used in the combinations of miniature trees made of jade and semiprecious stones, and Persian effects in the same way can be produced by using the colours found in the marvelous miniatures. But in all effects, colour intensity and relationship should be considered as most important.

V. MODERN FURNITURE

WHAT are the special features presented by modern furniture? How can our contemporary furniture be distinguished from furniture built many years ago? In reviewing the tremendous efforts that in recent years have been made both here and abroad, and in studying the photographs of modern furniture reproduced in this book, we may discover certain characteristics by which at some future date the work of today can be distinguished.

In analyzing the earmarks and special features presented by contemporary work, we should not be led to conclude that its place has been definitely established in the history of furniture design. Contemporary furniture is still in a state of transition. The mould is not yet hard. But certain features have already come forward and it will be possible to analyze the work of today by classifying many of its notable characteristics. The purpose of this analysis is not for cataloguing but rather that we may understand better what is being done and the reason for doing it.

Many questions come to our minds when we are inspecting furniture built today. When is furniture modern and when is furniture not modern? How is one to determine its origin? Who is the designer? Have we an individual piece of cabinet work before us or just another factory-made machine product?

We do not only desire to look at the surfaces presented by the model before us but we must try to penetrate and analyze what is before us. We not only desire to see what is inside and the method of construction but we wish to know what the spirit was that prompted its creation. This spirit of creation is one of the main guiding factors and much depends upon it. Anything designed with the intention of copying, either in detail or as a whole, works of past periods can hardly come under the heading of modern furniture.

On the other hand, the classical period styles cannot be swept off the map with one stroke. We should make a thorough study of the historical styles of period furniture so that we may begin where others left off. The best designers will, of course, be influenced by past styles but their interpretations will be individual and new. New pictures can be painted by an old brush and new tunes played on an old fiddle. The past must ever remain in the realm of history and the creative efforts of today must brush away the dust of ages and build in the spirit of our own time. But the artist of vision will not only be part of his own time but will project and indicate, in his work, the spirit of the future.

One of the typical characteristics of furniture of previous periods has been the shape of the leg. This was more or less a decorated structural support, as shown by the illustrations below. In most pieces, the leg was carried only as far as the knee of the piece of furniture, and here it was interrupted by the case or seat. In contrast to this, the furniture leg of today runs straight through to the hip. This not only adds grace, but it also gives it a constructive value by reinforcing the upper sections of the piece in question, and giving a unified solidity to the entire cabinet or other piece of furniture. It also adds a slender grace to the supporting members. The elongated, straight, slightly shaped, and extremely graceful leg is one of the new characteristics of furniture of today.

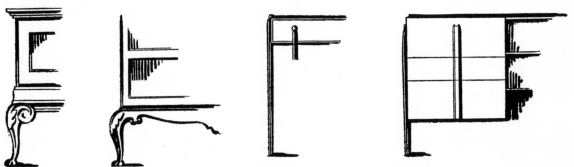

Old and new buffets, showing the difference in the structure of the legs.

Continuity of line is another aim of the modern furniture designer. In the designing of chairs, this is often expressed by the arm and leg being all in one uninterrupted curve. Often the back frame is continued and made one with the seat rail.

The modern designer avoids as much as possible the squaring off of surfaces by means of panelling or framing. The tendency today is against framing. Instead of sinking a picture into a frame, we endeavour to set the frame in back of the picture, similar to the old art of carving cameos. The flat surface is our aim. Modern wood-working machines and new technical processes enable us to build up large flat unbroken surfaces. Carving may be used but it will be used sparingly and with great restraint. It should not be employed as a means of ornament, but it may, to advantage, be used as an accent or key-note much as a scarf-pin may add distinction to a plain necktie.

Mouldings should be sharp and keen, giving a strong contrast of light and shadow expressive of speed, compression and the directness of modern life. The soft, flowing, sentimental mouldings that for many years we have copied from Greek temples are quite meaningless when used in modern furniture design. These antique mouldings were originally designed to silhouette against the sunny skies of Greece, and they lose their life when copied in wood and brought indoors. Curved mouldings may be used in metal work to give very effective results, because of the brilliant highlights on their pol-

38

ished surfaces. But wood mouldings used in furniture and interior decorations get a strong modern effect only when cut in sharp angles.

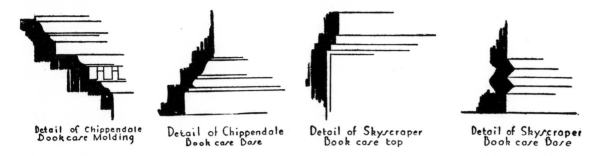

Detail of Chippendale Bookcase Molding

Detail of Chippendale Book case Base

Detail of Skyscraper Book case top

Detail of Skyscraper Book case Base

In modern furniture, the stamp of the creator is mostly quite apparent. He stands out from the creation and tells us at once the kind of man he is. When we talk to it, it will answer in French, German, Czechoslovakian, Dutch, Scandinavian, and perhaps even in English. The character of the creator is as difficult to hide as a light under a bushel basket.

Modern pieces of furniture can easily be grouped into several types or categories. Perhaps the simplest and most comprehensive classification would be to divide our modern pieces geographically according to the country of their origin. Another grouping, however, would recognize them as coming from the ranks of either architects, stage designers, or dressmakers. These are the three main classes and it is not difficult, once we know the key, to recognize to which group a particular piece of furniture belongs. Each has its distinctive characteristics.

The architect's furniture presents a certain element of line that is structural and it also represents an effort to emphasize the characteristics of the material of which it is made. It is often quite heavy and massive. It has bulk and three dimensions, besides being greatly influenced by the architectural features of the day.

When the stage designer or painter attempts to build furniture, he will try to achieve with colour and surface decoration what the architect is expressing with light and shadow and in three dimensions. His furniture is much more two-dimensional and has a tendency to over-state the surfaces,—that is, give the surfaces too much importance—and to over-decorate.

On the other hand, furniture designed by the stage designer has the virtue of being less hampered by limitations of construction. It is less traditional and in this way many original effects result from an apparent disregard of constructive features.

The dress designer attempts to clothe a room as he would drape a lady, using tassels on his furniture in place of handles, and over-refining his detail. He will attempt to finish details as though they were for a piece of jewelry by making his knobs of carved ivory and using enamel work and other ornaments of this type with his furniture. The introduction of very fancy tropical veneers by the French furniture designers is a good example of this type of creation. This type of furniture designer would not hesitate to use loosely woven materials and dress silks for furniture coverings. He would give a good deal of attention to surface and effects of colour but would be quite likely to neglect important constructive necessities of his furniture, as well as many other practical considerations.

Each of these three groups has its virtues and each has its shortcomings. If modern furniture is to take a permanent place beside period pieces there is one chief requirement necessary. This requirement is perfection. *Perfection not alone in design, but also in cabinet work and in finish.* A pleasing colour, as well as a pleasing design and attractive finish, may give a piece of furniture a smart appearance, but none of these will endure the acid test of time. If the cabinet work is not perfect, the furniture will not last. Good design, well balanced proportions, excellent cabinet work and perfect finish all combined in one piece of furniture are something quite rare and not to be seen every day. The reason for this is simple. The production of a piece of furniture combining all these virtues requires a good deal of time and attention. One is often asked why there is so little good modern furniture constructed in America today. This question may be easily answered. As long as the very first considerations in ordering an original piece of furniture are—How much will it cost? And when can it be delivered?—as long as these questions are foremost, it becomes almost impossible to create in the only spirit in which real art can be created. The only spirit in which real art can be created is expressed in the old phrase, "Art for art's sake."

The original conception of a piece of furniture, that germ in the creator's mind that begins building something which will result in a finished artistic work, is in no way different from the original germ that prompts the creation of any other artistic work. It is not unlike a song or a poem. It is inspired and its inspiration is not guided by dollars and cents. The same honesty that is required for the conception is also necessary for the execution. There should be consistency between the original idea and the carrying out.

Furniture, to be enduring, requires patience and time. The greatest mistake one can make is to hurry the cabinet-maker. It is very much like trying to make the potter's wheel turn faster than it does. It is not possible for either designer or layman to instruct the cabinet-maker regarding the length of time that his wood should be seasoned and finished. Wood poorly seasoned will soon warp and hideously distort the furniture. Time cannot be saved in this any more than it can be saved by hurried workmanship in making the joints or in matching the veneers.

The outward simplicity, as expressed in a plain surface, does not at all imply that this effect is created by a simple construction. Quite often a very simple surface represents the height of skilled cabinet work. In many cases, this plain surface is obtained by as much as five or more layers of wood running in opposite directions, constructed on a core bed, which has been prepared of many narrow strips glued together with much care and skill.

Simple surfaces are often quite deceptive. Their construction must be carefully planned by the designer and often inspected during the process of building. But these are not the only features that must be watched very carefully in the working out of new furniture models. More or less important changes often occur in the working out of the design. These changes are not due to lack of foresight and often occur to the most skillful designer. A piece of furniture drawn on paper is quite different from the same piece when it is ready to leave the shop and enter the finishing room. The play of light, the shadows, the bulk, and many other special features, become evident only after the piece has been constructed. Because of this, the very best results can only be obtained by first making a test model for observation. From this model the finished piece of furniture can be built with greater perfection.

After many visits to a cabinet maker's shop, a very striking conclusion may come to you, and that is, strange as it may sound, that most well-built pieces of furniture have a greater æsthetic appeal and look better before leaving the wood-working shop than after coming out of the finishing room. We are led to conclude that the finishing room does more harm than good. While it adds a finish and gives a certain final touch that we consider necessary, it robs the furniture of many virtues. Wood in its natural state still retains some of the life of the tree from which it was cut. This life is covered over by layers of paint and varnish and its natural characteristics are lost completely. While the wood remains unfinished, one can easily distinguish its species even without being a great expert in the knowledge of woods. This is easily accomplished by the colour, the grain, the surface, and other natural qualities presented by the wood under consideration. The charm, however, of natural wood depends on its light-absorbing quality. It is this that gives the velvety sheen to the dull surface. But the appeal of a fine bit of wood is not alone to the eye but also to the touch. A plain

41

surface of unfinished wood feels entirely different from the same wood treated and varnished.

If we are eager to preserve the beautiful and natural qualities of wood, we must conclude that the wood which is finished best is that which is finished least. The smallest amount of finish that we can possibly put on the surface of the wood and preserve it sufficiently from climatic changes and the grit of dust and dirt is a plain hard wax-rubbed finish. This is obtained by applying wax to the surface repeatedly, not once or twice but many times. There is nothing modern in this type of finish. It is perhaps the oldest of all our known surface coverings, but it still remains the most satisfactory. It is slow and its results are not immediate, but it is the safest and surest way to obtain a beautiful finish. A finish that is really beautiful will not grow less beautiful in time but will be enhanced by age. It will seem to grow richer year after year. It is also possible, before applying the wax finish, to tone the wood by a few coats of linseed oil which has been made thin with turpentine and perhaps faintly tinted. This oil and free-flowing pigment is easily absorbed in the fibre and structure of the wood and helps preserve the surface. A very good formula for making wax to be used in this connection is to mix equal parts of beeswax, resin and shellac and dissolve them all in hot turpentine.

Let us see what happens to a piece of furniture when it is sent to the finishing shop of today. The very first step in the operation is to clog up the pores of the wood with a filler or chemical. This same process applied to a living animal would cause ultimate death. And destroying the pores of a wood surface extinguishes that last flicker of life that remains in it from the tree.

There is a difference in light reflection between finished wood surfaces and unfinished surfaces. The finished surface reflects light, while the unfinished wood absorbs light. Wood that is stained suffers from a loss of character. The stain penetrates the surface and changes the natural colour of the wood. This tends to produce an uneven effect which makes it difficult for us to name the species of the wood. In contrast to stained surfaces, a new process has recently come to us for applying colour to wood by dyeing it under extreme pressure. Special dyes are employed for this process which penetrate the wood throughout quite in the same manner as cloth is dyed. The advantage of this process over the ordinary staining and finishing method is that the pores of the wood are not clogged by the dye and, in this way, a good deal of the life of the grain is preserved.

Painted and lacquered surfaces represent an art of their own. This art has found

42

its highest development in the marvelous achievements of Chinese and Japanese craftsmen. The furniture designer of the present day takes a good deal of delight in lacquering many surfaces of his creations. The modern furniture movement, which has come much to the fore in recent years, presents a great variety of painted and lacquered pieces. These have now taken an important place of their own.

In the finishing process, the air brush, which sprays paint evenly, has been found a great aid. A good lacquer finish requires at least five coats of pigment evenly applied. When each coat is thoroughly dried, the surface must be rubbed carefully with powdered pumice and crude oil. The simpler the surface and the less decoration it contains the more difficult it will be found to obtain a perfect finish. This is because small imperfections are easily concealed by the decorations. The best lacquer work can be produced only on close-grained wood and metals.

A chair does not have to be invented over again. But in designing a new model we must bear in mind that people sit differently today than they did a hundred years ago. The stiffness and formality of the early days have given way to more natural positions of repose.

The comfortable chair may be achieved in two ways: either with a shallow, rather high seat and high back, or with a decidedly low seat of great depth and comparatively low back. Our tendency toward the informal in all things makes the low, deep seat preferable.

Loose seat cushions add to the comfort. Tufted upholstery has given way to plain surfaces accentuating the line of construction and the beauty of the fabric used. All fringes, tassel edging and galloons are in the discard. If the lines of the chair are simple, its beauty may be enhanced with a figured covering. But if the lines of the chair are of shapely construction, this feature of the chair can be shown to the greatest advantage by the use of a plain covering.

Only a comfortable chair is beautiful. The first and last test for a chair is to sit in it.

Regarding tables, a few words of general principles may suffice. The general opinion that the standard height of a table is thirty inches should not be accepted as a law. The height of a table is proportionate to its length and width. It must also be consistent with the chairs which are to be used with it.

As a rule, low tables have an air of comfort while high tables, as is true of all other pieces of furniture, give the appearance of formality. Small incidental tables should always be decidedly low.

Tables give the modern designer a special opportunity of showing his skill in the construction and treatment of surfaces. The legs, as a supporting base, should be constructed in a way to interfere least with the comfort of the person sitting at the table. The top of the table may give the designer a chance to match beautifully grained woods or lend itself to much variety of treatment but its practical use must always be uppermost. Glass tops intended solely for the protection of the wood surface are highly objectionable. On the other hand, heavy slabs of half inch plate glass, especially with mirrored back, introduce a new and distinctive decorative element when used in this connection. Mirrored table tops are used frequently on modern furniture because they give a brilliant note and help bring a sparkle of light into the room; at the same time they reduce the woodiness and massiveness of the table. In planning the dimensions of a table, we should avoid making them too wide for it is not the length but the width of a table that makes for clumsiness.

In the designing of cabinets, dressers and side-boards, the decorative element can be expressed in accentuating the frame work and the structural features. If these features are not regarded, then a special treatment of the surfaces will bring forward a pleasing result. In other words, more care should be given to the finish and treatment of a surface if structural elements have been neglected. This can best be illustrated by comparing period pieces with the work of contemporary artists. In details like drawers or doors, it will be noticed that old pieces have these usually framed and sunk-in, while the modern tendency is to set the frame back, avoiding panels and bringing forward the flush surfaces of the drawers and doors.

Meaningless ornaments should be avoided as much as possible. Restraint is a very important factor in modern design. There are very few ornaments and embellishments which have much meaning to us, and therefore when there is any doubt they should be omitted. The design itself should be sufficient to provide an interesting play of light and shadow and make a pleasing appeal to the eye. If a design does not do this, then special decorations will hardly save the situation. Beautifully matched veneers, inlaid woods and marble tops are only appropriate in pieces of furniture that are extremely severe and simple in design. Cabinets and bookcases have recently been influenced by American skyscrapers. This new departure, representing the towers and set-back architecture of modern building, has become known by the name of skyscraper furniture. It has recently come forward to take its place with other modern furniture designs, and is clearly illustrated in this volume by several examples.

VI. MODERN LIGHTING FIXTURES

THE problem of lighting is certainly one of the oldest problems that humanity has faced. In this regard man can be said to be quite different from other animals. There was once an amusing definition given of man. It said that man was an animal who wore clothes, cooked and laughed. No other animal has these accomplishments but the definition could be made complete by saying that man uses artificial lighting. From the days of the caveman to the very latest electrical forces developed in Schenectady, lighting has been one of man's knottiest problems. Many have been the changes in our methods of lighting. Almost each generation in each country has made its contribution to this field. A catalogue of the many forms used by the different ages of man would almost show the progress of his civilization. It would include innumerable shapes of candlesticks, Roman lamps carved of stone, bronze church lamps for burning olive oil, oil lamps with wicks protected by glass globes—in fact, an almost unlimited variety of light-bearing utensils, as well as many changes in the lights themselves.

To come to our own era, it is not so very many years since the gas mantle came forward with its brilliant light; and gas is still used in many places for lighting purposes. But the greater efficiency of the electric bulb has, for the most part, displaced illuminating gas as a means of lighting. The development of our electric light has been most revolutionary. Here the problem of compression has been solved completely and safely. There is hardly any other field of human endeavour where so satisfactory an achievement has been made. Since the day of its birth, it has seen little or no change except in detail. The electric bulb is so simple and we have become so accustomed to its presence that we switch it on and off hardly giving it a moment's thought. If we were, however, to reflect, most of us would be somewhat surprised to realize the great and varied advantages of this cold light. By its use, smoke and the dangers of open flames have been entirely eliminated. Heat has been reduced to a negligible quantity. It is odourless and clean, and another advantage that immediately presents itself is the fact that, while an open flame uses great quantities of oxygen from the air, the enclosed light of an incandescent bulb uses none. In short, it has made all other sources of artificial light seem almost primitive. In the twisted wire of a vacuum bulb there has been condensed and concentrated the lighting power of two hundred or more candles. It is much more flexible than any other modern contrivance, for, without materially increasing its volume, a bulb can be adjusted to give almost any range of lighting force from the low light of one candle-power to the glare of several hundred candle-power.

Before leaving this subject, a word should be said for the old-fashioned candle. In many ways this form of light, with its sympathetic glow, has never been rivalled. It is extremely limited and has many disadvantages but it does something that no other form of light can do—it lends festivity to the home and gives a mystic air to the altar. The soft, flickering light caused by candles is always a sympathetic one. It will be a long time before the mellow light of candles at a dinner table is completely banished from the home.

While we are ready to admit the great achievement of the modern electric bulb, we must certainly deplore the lack of originality shown in our lighting fixtures. It seems as if all our engineering cleverness had been exhausted by the bulb and none had remained for the fixture. Perhaps the reason for this is simple. Engineers had done exactly what they wanted to do with the electric bulb but, when it came to fixtures, they did not seem to know what they wanted to do. The problems here are intricate and offer much variation. They are certainly still open for our engineers to solve. But the problem cannot be solved in a sentimental way. While a good deal of sentiment is expressed in the light of a flickering candle and also in the silken shade and soft glow of the oil lamp, which seems full and round like the lines of its own jar, there is little beauty or sentiment in the glowing twisted wires sealed in a vacuum bulb. This concentrated force must be directed and controlled. Perhaps the first people to understand the use of this form of lighting were the stage decorators of our day. They used lights to paint the stage pictures. The decorator of today, on the other hand, seems trying to soften it, to make it seem other than it is, in fact to deal with it sentimentally. He keeps trying in all manners and by all means but so far with very little success.

Let us again look back for a moment and this time recall from the recent past the history of our electric chandelier. At first, the electric chandelier was anchored in the center of a gingerbread plasterwork ceiling. It was elaborate and gaudy and hung with stones and crystals and all kinds of trinkets. It was a kind of Christmas tree made of metal and coloured glass. It gave light to itself and it also lit up the beautiful painting and coloured plaster-work on the ceiling. It lifted the head and eye upward and gave a very busy and unrestful atmosphere.

With the removal of the gingerbread decorations from our ceilings, there seemed little or no call for the central chandelier. Ceilings suddenly grew plainer and simpler and the conventional chandelier found no parking place on this plain surface. Of course, some of the decoration from the ceiling came down to the walls, for it wasn't possible in one stroke to do away with the entire idea of decoration. Wall papers were replaced by panelled walls and panelled walls called for small chandeliers, which we now term wall brackets, to relieve the flatness and give light. While these side lights were in a way a step forward and had certain great advantages to their credit, they still have the main defect of the central chandelier, and that is, they give a restless and distracting effect to the room. Your eyes are seldom at rest in a room fully lit by wall brackets, for each lamp in the path of vision seems to reflect in the corner of your eye.

Now a third step forward has been taken. The modern tendency for extreme simplicity has attacked the walls of our living rooms and the paneled mouldings are now taken off, giving a plain surface to a solid wall. This plain surface without panels or frames seems to ask for something different than the conventional side light. Something different must be devised.

If the light is to be removed from the ceiling and also from the wall, then the question at once arises:—Where should our light come from? The question can be answered in two ways, for after careful consideration, we find there are only two satisfactory forms of lighting. Either may be used or both may be used together.

The two forms of satisfactory lighting are, first, a direct and concentrated and, at the same time, portable light that can be adjusted to the book or work on the table or desk and one that is completely shielded from our eyes; and secondly, an indirect light that is best used for the general lighting of a room and is concealed and reflects its glow by flooding the entire ceiling. Its intention is not to light the ceiling but to use the ceiling as a reflector. This flood light, which should always be placed above the level of the eye, can be concealed in various ways. It requires none of the old-time lighting fixture paraphernalia or shades. It requires only an efficient reflector. It may be concealed in a new type of cornice board finishing off the top of a curtain. In this case, the lights should be so arranged that they reflect from the ceiling and also throw some of their light straight down along the curtain.

This idea of having the light at night come from the window has many advantages. As a room is planned, the source of light is one of the main things that should be considered. The character of a room will be better retained if the light in the daytime and at night comes from the same direction. This method of lighting will also show up the curtains at night to their best advantage.

There are many ways of concealing lights that are designed to flood the ceiling and give it indirect lighting. The *Ile de France*, the new French liner, has solved many of its lighting problems in a very ingenious and successful manner. Reflectors are concealed on the tops of cabinets and in the bowls of large urns that stand above the level of the eye and the light is cast from these hidden sources upon the ceiling. The effect is quite successful and results in a soft, pleasing and diffused light.

When the light is needed in a given place, movable fixtures must be employed. In order that this light shall be concentrated, these fixtures should be as flexible and as simple as possible. They should consist mainly of an electric bulb, a metal reflector, and an adjustable stand. The metal reflector does away with the old-fashioned parchment or silk lamp shade and has many advantages. A certain amount of light strains through the silk and fringes of a silk shade and all the trimmings that surround it, and, while this in itself may make a pretty picture, it is hardly a suitable solution of the lighting problem. The metal shade is much less sentimental, but, properly styled, it is extremely expressive of the modern spirit. It gives sharp contrasts and angular, geometrical lines. Its forms are simple. It fully conceals and greatly intensifies the sources of light yet it throws the spotlight where it is desired, and, by so doing, at once becomes more practical and agreeable. It may be used as a spot or flood light not only giving brilliant lighting effects but also extremely interesting shadows.

At the present moment, the form of this type of lamp is hardly pleasing but this is only a problem in styling. There is no reason why this type of reflector cannot be made modern in aspect and attractive in appearance. The plain metal, which may be anything from brass to polished steel or silver, can be allowed to show, or it can be lacquered in contrasting colours. The forms and shapes can be flowing or angular. The solution is close at hand and the problem is one for the modern decorator. The age we live in could be called the age of metal. It is with this material that the solution of our lighting problems will, no doubt, be solved.

VII. THE BATH-DRESSING ROOM

OF course there are no period bathrooms that can be copied. Chippendale never designed a bathtub. This room is purely a product of modern civilization. There is little tradition behind it and we have used our own ingenuity in the development and planning of the modern bathroom. Perfection of technical appliances —all products of our machine age—has made the bathroom of today possible.

The bathroom in America has developed along entirely different lines than has the European bathroom. In Europe even today the bathroom is still considered a luxury and is reserved mainly for the upper classes. America has made the bathroom, as it has also made the motor car and other modern appliances, a necessity. It has taken it out of the luxury class and has made it a part of every home. Of course, our first problem in bringing the bathroom to the general public was to make it sanitary, practical and economical. While there were advantages that came from these engineering feats, there were also disadvantages. The first thing to happen was the extreme standardization of bathrooms. For this we are now world famous. As white has always been the symbol for cleanliness, white has become the standard colour. Tiled floors and walls, white ceilings, white porcelain or enamel tubs and equipment are its distinguishing features. Until very recently all bathrooms were quite similar in character.

When the battle of sanitation was won, and in this regard we jumped a hundred years ahead of Europe, we turned our attention to the technical difficulties involved. As soon as these were overcome, the next step was to express individual taste and personality, as well as beauty, in the bath-dressing room.

Reason soon told us that a thing sanitary could also be made attractive. White is no more sanitary than any other colour; it only looks so. We began to feel our bathrooms should really be more related to the home and should not resemble the hospital or the laundry. Very soon the European idea of luxury entered into the planning of our new bath-dressing room.

Instead of condensing this room into a space no larger than an overgrown closet, we are now giving it a fair proportion with a full sized window and everything else that belongs to a room. The idea of the window being the same as the other windows in the house is to avoid the objectionable appearance of the old-time narrow bathroom window from the outside of the house.

The location of the fixtures are now carefully planned by the architect and not left, as in former times, to the fancy of the plumber. The bathtub is usually set into a niche. This has two advantages: In the first place, it protects the bather from drafts, and, in the second place, it allows the tub to be closed off from the room by means of a curtain, which, by the way, need not be white but may be of a fabric which fits into the general scheme of things. This fabric may be rubberized or rubber-lined to protect it from the splash of water.

Bathtubs may also be partly sunk into the floor and faced on front and top with slabs of precious marble or onyx. By doing this, we avoid showing too much white of the tub itself. The day when bathtubs and sanitary equipment will be available in all colours is not very far off. In fact, it will be very difficult for bathtubs to remain white in a gayly-coloured world.

The washstand, a very important feature of any bathroom, should be treated in a similar way and made to correspond in character to the tub in the same room. The washstand also may be set into a niche, faced on top with marble, and closed in the front to hide the unæsthetic plumbing features. An attractive mirror may be installed over the washstand where space is no object. The medicine chest should not be placed here but should be made a feature of its own.

As few medicine chests are large enough to hold all that they seem to require, it would be just as well to build one so proportioned that crowding would seem impossible. An attractive plan would allow for a full length medicine chest of about eighteen inches in width and a foot in depth. The door of this closet could be faced with a mirror and would extend down to the floor of the room. A companion closet to this, only built a little deeper, could be reserved for linen and towels.

Two main features of the modern bath-dressing room are an open fireplace and spacious dressing table. The flickering flame of an open fire gives an air of coziness and warmth. It also takes away from the utilitarian atmosphere that is set up by the tub and fixtures. The open fireplace in the bath-dressing room has a still further advantage in that it provides ventilation and reduces the moisture in the air.

The dressing table should be made to be the most personal piece in this room. Its colour scheme and design should give the main note for the decorations and the rest of the room should be well in keeping.

Regarding the floor, a variety of treatments is here possible. It may be made of marble, of various combinations of tiles, or it may be made of rubber. The base, however, should be of tile or marble and should run into the wall and be carried up as high as necessary. The walls may be finished in paint or papered with modern wallpaper. If the last treatment, however, is desired, it would be best to protect the paper from steam condensation by varnishing its surface. Where tiles are used half way up the wall, a very interesting effect may be gained by using paper above the tiling and clear across the ceiling. In such instances where there is no danger of water splashing against the paper, it is not necessary to protect it with varnish. The slight vapour in a bath room is easily absorbed by the paper on the wall and should not cause any trouble. The ceiling should, in any case, harmonize with the rest of the room.

If space permits, both a screen and lounge will be found valuable and attractive additions. Adjoining the modern bath-dressing room a properly ventilated water-closet should be placed.

In this way, the modern trend in decorating, which makes personal things impersonal and gives the most impersonal an air of the personal, is conquering a new field. Certainly the bathroom of the past has been most ordinary and quite impersonal. It expressed absolutely no individuality. The modern bath-dressing room, however, with its added luxuries and comforts and its soft, glowing lights, adds an intimate note to a much neglected and over-standardized part of the home.

VIII. AMERICAN CITY ARCHITECTURE

AMERICA today is the only country in the world that may be said to be creating a modern architecture that is distinctive and expressive of its people. A new note has been struck here and a creation as complete as the present one is rare in the history of the world.

We pass through the narrow chasm formed by towering skyscrapers and little realize the significance of these huge skyward masses. It often takes the admiration of others to make us appreciate the value of what we have. Especially when that admiration comes from Europe, the home of artistic culture, do we begin to take notice. Our main artistic character and our distinctive achievement in the eyes of foreigners is, no doubt, the skyscraper.

The skyscraper is a creation forced upon us by necessity. Its idea is in keeping with one of the main features of our time, and that is, compression. The skyscraper compresses space. The credit for this innovation goes to the distinguished architect, Louis H. Sullivan, who, over thirty years ago, in Chicago, was the first to conceive the idea of standing a building up on its side. He developed it vertically rather than horizontally. At first such a building seemed a freak, something for sightseers to visit, but soon it was recognized as an original achievement. Other skyscrapers followed, and the unaccustomed eye began, by educating itself, to see real beauty in skyscraper architecture.

The very first buildings which were constructed in this new vertical scheme of things consisted of a series of low buildings placed one upon the other. Classical forms were imitated. Rows of Greek columns were placed one over the other like layers in a complicated cake. Architecture was thus piled skywards. The problems forced upon us were met very adequately in the steel and other constructive features of the building, but when it came to the artistic consideration, when it came to design, our first attempts were to squeeze a new form into an old classical mould. Artistically this proved a failure. New forms require new designs, and new designs could not come from imitation.

The classical forms were soon found worthless for this type of structure. And even Gothic lines, which being vertical seemed to fit the form of the new structure, were not successful for the character of the new buildings. The Woolworth building, which was the tallest and perhaps the most daring structure of its time, is a good example of what we have in mind. It represents in its detail a faithful elongated copy of Gothic church architecture. The lines seemed to fit the form but the idea of a church on lower business Broadway seems incongruous. It is out of character. The design or

52

outward shell is not in keeping with the whole structure. Yet a Gothic church on lower Broadway is not more out of keeping than a Greek temple built in the heart of the city for the Pennsylvania Railroad station. Each in itself is a fine reproduction of a type of architecture, but, like all copies, it represents something that is dead—a civilization past, a life not our own.

Read what Mr. Frank Lloyd Wright says about this in an article entitled *The Architect and the Machine* in his series *In The Cause of Architecture,* published in the *Architectural Record:*

"Our 'technique' may therefore be said to consist in reproduction, imitation, ubiquity, a form of prostitution other ages were saved from, partly because it was foolish to imitate by hand the work of another hand. The hand was not content. The machine is quite content. So are the millions who now have, as imitations bearing no intimate relation to their human understanding, things that were once the very physiognomy of the hearts and minds—say the souls of those whose love of life they reflect. . . . Is it that we are now willing to take it in quantity too—regardless of inferior quality and take all as something canned—long ago? One may live on canned food quite well—but can a nation live a canned life in all the rudimentary animal expressions of that life? Indefinitely? Canned Poetry, canned Music, canned Architecture, canned Recreation. All canned by the machine. I doubt it, although I see it going on around me. It has its limits."

Surely there must be a solution to this evil. Architectural detail has become a thing meaningless and absurd. It is like the work of a giant pastry-cook, modelling nonsensical scrolls and dots over the outside of his cakes.

For this state of affairs Mr. Wright proposes the following solution:

"We must have the technique to put our love of life in our own way into the things of our life, using for our tool the machine to our own best advantage—or we will have nothing living in it at all—soon. How to do it? Well! How does anyone master tools? By learning the nature of them and, by practice, finding out what and how they do what they do best—for one thing. Let architects first do that with a machine. Architects are or must be masters of the industrial means of their era. They are or must be interpreters of the love of life in their era. They must learn to give it expression in the background for that life—little by little, or betray their office. Either that or their power as normal high priests of civilization in a democracy will never take its place where it is so badly needed. To be a mason, plasterer, carpenter, sculptor or painter won't help architects much—now."

53

The pastry-cook method of architectural design is fast vanishing. We are confronted with too many horrible examples to want to add more. The pomp and glory of this type of building has now vanished and has taken on a mean and petty aspect. The only period decoration that a modern skyscraper could have would be decoration of our own period and, in this regard, attempts are already under way. Civilization and architecture reflect each other.

Another penetrating interpreter of contemporary American civilization and architecture, Mr. Lewis Mumford, writing about this subject in his admirable little book *Sticks and Stones,* says:

"In the course of this survey, we have seen how architecture and civilization develop hand in hand: the characteristic buildings of each period are memorials of their dearest institutions. The essential structure of the community—the home—the meeting place, the work-place—remains; but the covering changes and passes, like the civilization itself, when new materials, new methods of work, new ideas and habits and ways of feeling, come into their own. . . . Occasionally the accidental result will be good, as has happened sometimes in our skyscrapers and factories and grain elevators; but an architecture that must depend upon accidental results is not exactly a triumph of the imagination, still less is it a triumph of exact technology."

Mr. Mumford also expresses the belief that, when the conditions are ripe for good architecture in America "the plant will flower by itself," as it did in the Middle Ages as well as during the Renaissance, and in the new garden-cities of England, Holland and Germany. He is also firmly convinced that one of the great frauds of our age is embodied in the notion that our architecture will be improved by courses of appreciation in our museums and colleges. Appreciation and application are different things and application that follows closely on the heels of appreciation is most often only imitation. And even worse than this. It is often copying something dead and trying to make it express something that should be alive.

While lack of space has pressed our buildings skyward, lack of time makes us hurry past. We have little time and certainly not enough leisure to enjoy the intricate designs on a building covered with architectural detail. In this respect, we are quite different from the generations which have preceded us. The city dweller of the past had a good deal more time at his disposal. He was able to promenade the streets and contemplate the motifs and charm of a fancy iron grill, or any of the other hundred features presented by the structures of the period. The modern city architect of today can hardly hope to have his work admired in all its detail by the general public. He must depend upon large masses, upon the three-dimensional forms, and not divert the attention to meaningless carved detail.

The buildings that we are beginning to notice are those which seem to be painted with a wide brush against a clear sky—a sky filled with great jagged masses of new attempts in architectural creations.

The characteristics of the building of the future will be those that are in keeping with the life of its time. The big masses will be brought out by sharp contrasts of light and shadow. The planes will not be flat but three-dimensional and cubic, and the colours will be sober and dignified.

The strong three-dimensional decorative element that is now becoming apparent in modern architecture will help a good deal to do away with the fragile two-dimensional surface decorations of the past. The art of the twentieth century could, in a way, be' said to be distinguished primarily by its effort and endeavour to eliminate superficial, unnecessary decoration. As a result of this, it has been bringing forward the natural beauty of the material used. It also is taking advantage of many modern constructive features that can be displayed in a decorative way.

Brick tapestries hung from the sky are as decorative as anything yet done on a large scale. Mosaics of coloured stones or tinted bricks are being used most effectively in this new art.

Other materials also are coming to the front. We have not yet learned how to use reinforced concrete or steel in an architecturally decorative way but the time is not far off when these new materials will take their places as things of beauty in themselves. New principles of construction may be found necessary, new standards to meet new uses and conditions, but these are already in the hands of architects and the time does not seem far off when new materials will be used in a variety of ways to achieve new architectural effects.

The new building law in New York City requiring the recessing of upper stories is a good example. It has broken the solid cube of the old type building into terraced units. The terraces in themselves are only a constructive necessity but, when well proportioned and designed, they add a good deal of interest and decorative value to the mass of the building. In a way, this can be said to be a happy accident, for our building ordinance in New York City was not originally introduced from artistic motives. It was prompted mainly by hygienic considerations. Its purpose was to provide more light and air and direct sunshine to the masses of people who were workers in the many offices that the buildings contain. It was an attempt prompted by necessity—

the necessity that demands more air and sun to penetrate the deep canyons of New York City.

At first architects feared that this new ordinance was a restraining force and would compel their creative work to take uninteresting channels. Many expressed the idea that pure imagination would be bound to suffer from a rigid rule that required buildings to be built in steps. But soon it was realized that the confinement was not so great and that the ordinance gave play to a great variety of original treatments expressive of our age.

At the present moment, there is a slow but steady architectural development along lines that are purely American. Some architects call this spirit in our new architecture the spirit of democracy, others call it the result of the machine age, and still another group of architects are content to allow it to remain the commercial spirit of our country. But these variations are only in name. The modern skyscraper is a distinctive and noble creation. It is a monument of towering engineering and business enterprise. It stands as a symbol of American life of today, much as the pyramids were symbols of the life of ancient Egypt.

New forms are being created and old ones destroyed. The whole process is still in a formative stage and for the moment only the main lines of our new architectural world are evident.

In this connection, it would be difficult to prophesy what will follow in the next few generations. At present a good many new buildings are looked upon as novelties and even freaks, or as necessary evils, for, when the problem of a new public building arises, there is still usually a complete return to the classical form.

Our museums, libraries and government buildings are still being constructed along classical lines. The reason for this is apparent. As public buildings are constructed to last for a great number of years, there is a feeling that the mode of today will be much altered and changed tomorrow and that the new architectural conceptions of today will be very old in a short while. It seems safer, therefore, though out of keeping, to adhere still to classical lines. But this idea is passing quickly and the birth of a new and distinctive American architecture is imminent.

This modern architecture which condenses space by a method of piling up, giving a three-dimensional interplay of cubic forms, has entered our civilization. It is bound to reflect its character upon the lives of those that live and work among the huge buildings. This reflection, in time, must alter the general public taste.

A certain consistency will be looked for, a certain matching of values and conditions, and our interiors, decorative arts and furniture design are already under the powerful modern architectural influence. This can only resolve into one thing: a decorative art that is in keeping with the country and the people who live in it. It will resolve into an American decorative art, original and at the same time satisfying. The result will be a new American period, the period of tomorrow certainly, if not of today.

IX. MODERN ART IN BUSINESS

MODERN art in business can be said to date from the decline of art patronage. As soon as artists became free from the old-world idea that art must be made to please those who supported the artists, then the artist began to support himself. And with this came art in business. When the artist was bored with the discomforts of poverty, he took on odd jobs in the fields of decorating, advertising and other very modern fields where his taste and ability could show themselves.

The artist of today is not unrelated to the business man. They have a basic idea in common and that is that they must both have a clear and keen understanding of modern humanity and human psychology. Enterprise, for both, depends upon this and, strange to say, modern art also must consider this factor.

The idea that an artist is only an artist and that a business man is no more than a business man belongs to a past date. There is a certain overlapping of interests. The business man must do something of the artist's work and the artist must concede a little and work with modern business. Perhaps this is the main reason why artists have discarded their velvet caps and Bohemian dreamers have become a race almost extinct and are at present mainly confined to fiction and scenes in the movies.

The modern artist is born in an industrial age in a country where there is great enterprise and activity, he is surrounded with commerce, industry, and great engineering and mechanical marvels. It is no longer possible for him to retreat into the solitude of an imaginative life. It is no longer possible for him to live in the dead past and yet to become part of the living world about him. And he wants to "belong." To belong to something of today.

At the same time, the modern business man also must be a little more than his title implies. He must be interested in other things besides his figures, which represent only dollars. The business man of today is more than a shop-keeper and he must be a good deal more to become a leader in his class.

There is a saying that the history of France could be written in the songs of the nation for these songs recorded the popular trend of events, and, art, as we said before, has always been the one record of its time. It has recorded each period of civilization. Therefore, if art is to record the business and industrial life of today, the artist must enlist himself in their service, be in close harmony with them.

The problems we face today are a deal different from those of the last generation. The main reason for this is the advent of the young infant known as the machine age. Machine production has replaced hand work to a very great extent and this has done away with the sacred traditions upheld by the proud craftsmen of the past.

The machine is very much like a young, crying child. It has very little past but faces a good deal of future. Its first event is the act of its being born. The first machine is only an invention and from this step it must be developed toward technical perfection.

At first the product of a new machine enters into direct competition with the product of hand work. Here the business man must step in and regulate such factors as price and quality. But, after these are achieved, the very next step in production must enlist the artist. Now appearance and style become an important factor. In this way art enters into the machine product.

After this step is accomplished, the business man again has something to say. For now he discovers that good forms sell much better and cost no more. The work of the artist has become profitable both in industry and in business. It has injured no one but has given the public something that looks better and is of greater value and at the same time it has earned a lucrative reward for all engaged in the enterprise.

This was first most evident in the field opened to the dress designer. The business prospered in direct relation to the ability of the artist. But this was quickly followed in almost every other field of endeavour. One by one, in rapid succession, new fields were thrown open—poster art, stage designing, window decorating, textiles, automobile and motor boat design, and even instruments like fountain pens and telephones fell into the hands of modern artists who try to express in their forms a new spirit—the spirit of today.

The modern designer must naturally be in close contact with the industrial development of his time. And, even more than this, he should have a little foresight so that he can see a few steps ahead, for his design of today will tomorrow be out of date unless it forecasts to a degree the future. It is also his duty to understand both the nature of the material used and the mechanical working of the product that he is designing. He will invent new forms just for pleasure in the enterprise.

New forms are not justified except by necessity. It is just as wrong to adhere to historic styles long outworn, as it would be to introduce decorations that are unnecessary and not in the spirit of today.

Style has become a vital factor in modern business. Some of the most enterprising business houses here and abroad have long recognized this fact and have engaged artists of repute to take charge of this vital factor in their business. In many cases policies have been established where all expenditures must be checked or directed along artistic channels. Such policies have not only been found enterprising but also profitable. Many houses have reaped rich harvests from innovations of this description, and, incidentally, have established for themselves reputations as leaders in their respective fields.

Not very many years ago modern business seemed to consist of having the latest labour-saving devices, the best systems of accountancy and the right competitive price. The most enterprising businesses of today have placed all these as secondary factors and brought into the foreground a modern artistic spirit. No detail in a modern business organization passes without the touch of the artist's hand. From the business card and letterhead of the firm to the fixtures, advertising, posters, and all the way through the entire structure of the industry to the product itself, an artistic expression prevails.

It would be an exaggeration to say that this is universally accepted, but it would be correct to say that the industries and business houses which seem foremost in their fields and most enterprising are giving their thought and consideration to modern art in connection with their enterprise. It would also be correct to say that the industries which seem tottering and about to dissolve are those which are paying no attention to the artistic factor. The original Ford car itself is a good example of this. The machine was good and was perfected to do the work for which it was designed, but without artistic consideration, it finally lost ground and all the engineers in America were unable to contribute any vital factor to recover the business. It was up to the artist to save the situation.

The machine has also become an educational factor as well as a force prompting artistic development. We can realize this easily if we look back into the history of photography. This history is not an old one. It is only a recent development. The camera is a modern machine. The early photographs tried to copy nature with very little success. The photographs of the early seventies showing family groups in rigid poses staring most unnaturally at the camera were hardly examples of art, nor did they copy nature very happily. This was caused both by lack of art and by the limitations of the machine; but with the introduction of snapshots and instantaneous exposures, this rigidity and static formality were soon broken down and we began to see the world fairly naturally through the mechanical eye of the camera. Snapshots of horse races showing a horse taking a hurdle with all four hoofs almost together at once contradict our old conception, which, no doubt, came from the sporting prints of a horse in motion. This is only one example of how the machine became an educational factor as well as a force in modern artistic development. There are many other examples but the point is quite evident and clearly illustrated in the field of photography. To this field still a third dimension was added by the motion picture, and this was again extended artistically in slow motion pictures showing the rhythm and grace of a movement from its start to its finish.

The machine even penetrates the surface of things and photography has not restricted itself to the mere record of what the eye could see. Its progress goes on. It has employed all available scientific forces in order to penetrate the surface of things and X-ray pictures are the result. Here we have a record of concealed matter and still another development would be the microscopic wonders of minute life not visible to the naked eye.

Other technical fields could tell a similar story. Photography, the product of a machine, is not alone in its remarkable progress and development. Art is not alone restricted to the brush of a Rubens or a Rembrandt or to any picture mounted in a gold frame, but it can also be achieved with the aid of the machine. The recognition of this fact would immediately bring us a long step forward, and it is necessary that we go a great deal forward because, in many ways, we have been quite backward.

The only reason why America was not represented at the exhibition of decorative industrial art held in Paris in 1925 was because we found that we had no decorative art. Not alone was there a sad lack of any achievement that could be exhibited, but we discovered that there was not even a serious movement in this direction and that the general public was quite unconscious of the fact that modern art had been extended into the field of business and industry. On the other hand, we had our skyscrapers, and at that very date (1925), they had been developed to such an extent that, if it had been possible to have sent an entire building abroad, it would have been a more vital contribution in the field of modern art than all the things done in Europe added together.

The skyscraper is certainly the monument of American business and American enterprise. This has struck the keynote of our civilization. The French exhibition had only one lesson that we could learn. There was nothing there that expressed the American spirit, but the lesson to be learned was that the same spirit indicated by the architecture in America was the spirit necessary for the interior development. Architecture and decorative art must go hand in hand. The outside and the inside must all be of one piece and of one spirit. This harmony can only be accomplished by bringing the same spirit into American decorative art as already has been brought into and successfully developed in our architecture.

X. *SOME PRACTICAL CONSIDERATIONS OF ART IN BUSINESS*

THE rise and development of modern art in business is so recent that its history is clear before us. The same principles that typify modern art in other fields are true in the field of business, but a few words of practical suggestion in a general way might be in place at this moment. We must again repeat our slogan and keep it ever before us;—"Decorating is eliminating." Eliminating is the essence of modern art in business.

Slight compromises may be made in other fields. Fantasy and other factors may be tolerated, but in business, art must be strict and severe. The principles are, straight lines, cold colours for backgrounds—such as grays, silver, black and light green—and sharp colour contrasts. These three essentials make modern art. There are other factors, as, for instance, diffused lighting and modern lighting fixtures (to which a chapter has been given) which are also of great importance, but the three essential factors remain: straight lines, cold colours for backgrounds and sharp colour contrasts. Let us see how these fit into the modern scheme of things? A modern store is a very complex organization. It takes the supervision of a person well trained in all the branches of modern art to introduce that expression in every channel of his organization. It is not alone a matter of styling. Neither is it only presenting the merchandise before an impressionistic background. An understanding of the importance of the various mediums at the disposal of a large organization is perhaps the most necessary requirement.

A great many stores would consider it an unnecessary expenditure to have their letterheads made by an artist of reputation in the field of typographic design. Yet this letterhead is the silent representative of the firm. This letterhead may reach many places that the merchandise may never reach. It is a little thing, but of great consequence.

A model letterhead should be simple and dignified. It should be well proportioned, not too black with printing material nor too light and feminine, excepting perhaps for a firm specializing in French perfume. It is decidedly bad taste to make a display of all the medals awarded to the firm's product, on this letterhead. Nor does it add greater dignity to a firm for the letterhead to list the addresses of its foreign offices. Clear writing and nice printing will add more style than a whole row of medals and a whole column of foreign offices. There are few letters received in a morning's mail that, in this regard, stand out in a truly dignified manner.

The show-window of a store should receive great consideration from an artistic point of view. In the majority of cases, the show-window is the greatest direct medium for advertisement in the possession of a concern. It speaks to the public without and silently invites them to closer inspection and to a visit inside. In a way it is like a stage and the street contains an audience ever passing before it.

Being like a stage, it must be flexible and easily adaptable to many types of settings. Changes must be made quickly and completely. It would, therefore, be a great mistake to introduce expensive wood or stone wainscotings as the background for this commercial stage. Such procedure would not allow for the necessary changes. The lighting also should be so arranged that, while concealed, it will allow for the greatest possible number of effects. Here again cast-iron fixtures and especially built-in lights should be avoided.

While a show-window is very much like a stage, it still should not be too stagey; nor should it produce too home-like an atmosphere. It should be impersonal and adaptable to the merchandise for which it is a background. This background, so to speak—for it is also a foreground—should not tend to cheapen the merchandise and, at the same time, it would be equally wrong to present the goods in an atmosphere that looked so exclusive as to scare off the possible purchaser. Of course, the colour schemes should vary according to the type and character of merchandise shown.

Each kind of merchandise presents its own problem, and it would be impossible within the limits of this space, to provide suggestions for each particular type of merchandise. But a few schemes may be suggested so that the worker in this field may have several definite examples of modern displays.

Each kind of merchandise calls for a special type of background. For instance, leather goods and luggage will show up most harmoniously against a background of tan, brown and henna, while evening gowns can be most effectively displayed against silver, gray and black. The reason for this is because leather goods do not require a cold background but one that blends with the merchandise shown. In the case of evening gowns, decided contrasts are called for. The neutral and cold colours will allow the gowns to "sing out" and stand forward. At the same time, small objects, such as hand bags, jewelry, etc., can best be displayed in a window that is very shallow and of which the floor is slightly raised. The reason for this is quite obvious. Small objects require closer inspection and should be nearer the eye of the observer. Too many small objects in a window will defeat their own purpose for they tend to create too worried or busy an effect. On the other hand, a Palm Beach display requiring various mannequins and an outdoor sunny atmosphere clearly calls for a low floor and a deep setting. Above all, the show window must be flexible, for each type of merchandise has its own potentialities and each type can be shown in a variety of ways in combination with numerous schemes. The more flexible the stage the greater the possibilities.

Possibilities and copied settings do not make for good windows. There is a secret that must be learned before windows will appeal and this secret is the art of giving life to the scheme presented, of which the merchandise is a part. There are modern windows that follow all the rules but still appear dead and wooden, and there are also modern windows that seem to break all the rules but arrest your attention at each detail. How is one to put life into objects that seem dead? This surely cannot be achieved by what is commonly known as "window trimming," nor can it be achieved by crowding as much stuff into the window as it will hold. Merchandise must be carefully selected for purposes of display. Choosing merchandise for a window is almost an art in itself. Two gowns may each in itself be stunning and the very latest in fashion but when placed side by side they will clash and form an ugly combination. Colour, texture and design are factors to be considered in the selection of merchandise to be displayed. Their combined effects must be visualized and made appropriate for the setting and general scheme which, in many cases, may be made up of a background of incidental pieces of furniture. But even the pieces of furniture must be appropriate in order that life may not be lost. In showing crinoline dresses, they may be displayed against a period background, but modern gowns certainly call for modern settings and, for this reason, period furniture would hardly fit into an ultra-evening gown display. The same that is true of furniture would also be true of the background and the other properties of this glamorous and talking stage.

Let us leave the show-window and enter into the shop itself. Here we are confronted with new problems. Each shop presents a problem that must be solved in a different way, but in all cases the spirit of the solution should be modern. The greatest mistakes made in decorating a shop are usually made in the original planning.

In planning a store, it is extremely important that one scheme of things prevail. A certain unity is necessary. This unity must be expressed in a direct and simple manner. Trying to introduce too many ideas into one shop is even worse than being devoid of any ideas.

The problem of the specialty shop is rather typical and can best serve as an instructive example. These shops are usually narrow in frontage but run rather deep. They get their light usually from the street in front but this light is more often than not cut off by the show-window. Sometimes this type of shop has daylight also entering from a court in the rear but, in most cases, this source of light is also cut off by partitions, offices or store-rooms. In other words, the average specialty shop is a long stuffy place that has daylight at both ends but with this daylight usually blocked out. What is the result? The result is dreary. The shops seem dead and the atmosphere very stuffy and uninviting.

How can this best be avoided? The problem is not difficult. First of all, the windows in the back court should be kept clear and storage and office space found somewhere else. Also the show-window in front should be made part of the shop itself. This can easily be accomplished by taking off the back. This would open the shop, so to speak, from end to end between the glass of the show-window and the glass of the windows facing the court. A certain sparkle and intimacy is immediately gained and people passing in the street are often more attracted to the shop itself than to the selections made for the show-window. Shops that are thus arranged immediately become more inviting and less formal in their character.

While this scheme of things is possible nine times out of ten, it cannot be laid down as a cast-iron rule, for there are shops that require individual treatment and too much generalizing would be dangerous. But in the main the above solution has proved most satisfactory.

Show-cases and counters present still another problem for the long narrow store. In most cases, they are lined up on either side of the wall, making the central space but a narrow aisle and forcing all movement in one up and down direction. It not only makes it difficult for people to pass each other but it gives the shop, which is already too long, an appearance of being twice as long. This is a common error and can easily be rectified by allowing the cases to stand out from one wall only and making the passage on the other side of the store. Combinations or groups of mirrors arranged opposite the show cases will give the appearance of a much wider establishment.

A pleasant atmosphere and attractive groups of furniture are quite essential to this type of shop. A modern shoe-store should not have rows of chairs, reminiscent of a third-class motion-picture house, lined up along the walls, but it should rather use short settees and occasional tables, arranged in various nooks and combined with display cases and mirrors appropriate for shoes. Here again lighting presents a very important problem. In the case of this type of shop, the lights should be concealed as much as possible. They should be diffused and, at the same time, cheerful, and they should also show up the merchandise to its best advantage. In other words, it is quite sensible to arrange the lights in a shoe-store so that shoes will get the light and not hats. While the

65

importance of proper lighting and lighting fixtures has long been recognized in the home, stores and offices are very much behind the times. Very often little or no lighting adjustment is made by the new tenant, who seems very ready to accept the fixtures provided by the building for the office or shop, while the same tenant would arrange for his own lighting fixtures at home. Individual lamps give a feeling of intimacy and charm which is a great advantage in the high-class specialty stores.

The modern spirit does not mean necessarily that the furnishings must be up to the last minute in style. There must be a relation between the furnishings and the type of merchandise to be displayed. An ultra-modern background would hardly suit a shop stocked with conservative merchandise and there are some shops that are, by their nature, conservative. A men's furnishings shop could be very up-to-date and best furnished in the modern manner by adhering strictly to conservative colours and avoiding anything that looks too freakish. At the same time, the department selling ladies' sport clothes should have a background of bright and cheerful colours in order to give the feeling of outdoors. Here again it is most important to avoid effects that are too theatrical or novel. There is great danger in making a shop look like a night club. And here again the decorations of the shop, like the decorations of the show-window, should be kept as flexible as possible. In this field of decoration, things cannot be done for eternity. This is contrary to the modern idea and to the spirit of our age. The best we can do is to provide adequately and attractively for the moment. The reason for this would soon become clear if one were to think of the tremendous speed expressive of our times. The new hats of today are the old hats of tomorrow. Styles change rapidly. Types of merchandise alter enormously and public taste demands a flexible and a not too rigid merchandising organization. No intelligent buyer will stock up for a long period of years, no matter how attractively the merchandise presents itself. New merchandise demands new backgrounds. Backgrounds should not be built for eternity because they must provide for the constant changes in merchandise. They are built for one purpose and that is to show off the merchandise attractively. And when the merchandise changes they themselves must also change.

The modern department store presents a problem that is not in some ways unlike the problem of a modern city. A store-planning department not unlike a city-planning department should be installed. While the merchandising manager of a large department store has been specially trained in merchandising methods as well as economic conditions, the manager of the planning department must assume full responsibility for all present and future developments, both from the utilitarian and the artistic viewpoints. He must also understand the traffic problems with which every large department store is confronted, and, at the same time, he must also be in close touch with new ideas developing in Europe as well as ideas in his own country. A capable architect should be in charge of the planning and all questions in this field should be referred to him. At the present time, the method of department store procedure is rather deplorable. The tactics of today seem to be that of copying. Each shop imitates what it sees in the next shop. Very few work on systematic, distinctive plans of their own. The reason for this is quite clear. Modern competitive methods are rather sharp and keen and, while the average window dresser in whose charge store-planning is often placed is capable of imitation and copying, he is not equipped to do any creative work in his field. The department store systematically working out its own plans in all its fields of endeavour, from its letterhead to the show-window, from its flags and holiday decorations to its annual January white sale, would soon build for itself a prestige distinctive and profitable. Many department stores are beginning to recognize this and have made attempts in one or more directions, but no store in America has accomplished it throughout the entire organization. And the first store that will introduce modern art into its woof and warp will be destined to gain great distinction as well as valuable prestige.

XI. THE INFLUENCE OF PEASANT ART

DURING the last fifty years there has been a steady decline in craftsmanship. The old guild traditions which form the foundation of craftsmanship are now almost entirely lost.

The great wave of industrialism has swept over the civilized countries and washed away individual workmanship. In a few isolated centres, far removed from intellectual and industrial cities, some of the traditions of fine craftsmanship are still preserved. In the mountains of Austria-Hungary, in the fiords of Norway and in the north country of Sweden, we find the traditions still maintained. Standardization and the other mechanical earmarks of our civilization have only to a slight degree entered these remote artistic civilizations. In many sections great efforts are being made to preserve the traditional arts of the localities. For instance, the remote little country of Iceland is doing all it can to preserve its national artistic traditions. The Government has arranged for free courses of lessons in wood carving where national designs are copied and old models preserved. The state contributes a thousand crowns a year to this venture. In Sweden, as far back as 1600, steps were taken to preserve the local characteristics of the costumes in different parts of the country, and it is because of some of these measures that we can today find costumes made recently which retain the wonderful glamour and mediæval character of their ancestors. The remarkable thing is that women's dresses have changed oftenest in the highly civilized and industrialized centres of the world. The peasant costumes of today are faithful reproductions of their original type. This is more true of women's dresses than it is of the costumes of men, which have been more easily influenced by the changing fashions of various times.

In certain localities, the clergy and the elders of the parish hold a rather strict control over the clothes of their community. Shoe-makers and tailors are warned not to make clothes in any other fashion than that of their own locality. A definite pride in their ancestry keeps up these quaint traditions. A certain honour in belonging to a particular locality helps preserve and establish home arts and craftsmanship.

Art is at all times like a pendulum, swinging from one extreme to another, unless, of course, it is held in check by superstitions and the twenty-four traditional Swedish elders. But disregarding the extremes to which art can go and the left and right swing of the pendulum, there are certain characteristics which remain true for all crafts.

The great ideal sought for by most craftsmen is naturally perfection, perfection mainly of a mechanical kind. But this perfection is the sole virtue, though artistically it may be said to be a vice, of the industrial product. The sewing machine, for instance, sews much better mechanically than a needle and thread in the fingers of a skilled worker, though artistically it has never wholly displaced the hand product. Machines have been invented for turning wood, for pressing patterns into leather, for weaving lace, and stamping out all kinds of objects used in daily life. Perfection has been gained, labour has been reduced, and time has been saved, as well as expenditure, but, alas, the individual touch, the secret of craftsmanship, is lost. The entire industrial world, all the ingenious inventions, and all our clever devices put together, cannot give the individual touch that is so appealing and, at the same time, so artistically desirable. That is why an artistically sensitive person will always choose the hand-gathered and hand-woven stuff in preference to the more perfect fabric gathered and woven by a machine.

The difference between machine-made and hand-made products is mainly in the objects that lie behind them. A machine displays no intelligence of its own but it reproduces and imitates without any diversions the intelligence of its inventor. Its object is to continue reproducing and making the same thing over again. The peasant, however, lives in close touch with nature. His work lies in the fields and hills of his native abode. His struggle for existence is usually confined to the summer months. Four or five long winter months of comparative idleness come upon him. It is during these times that he gets out his knife and other simple tools and his ability as an artist comes to the fore. His mind, while simple, is filled with three-dimensional forms. All forms of nature are three-dimensional. Bulk is an important factor in peasant art. His ability as an artist springs from natural desires. He is not pressed by time, neither is he prompted by commercialism. The result is naturally something of fine craftsmanship and of individual taste. In form and pattern traditional characteristics may be seen but, unlike the product stamped out by the machine, no two specimens of peasant work can be said to be alike.

In our intellectual centres, where guild traditions and craftsmanship have sunk to the low level where we find them today, the artist is no longer a supreme craftsman. He has become in a way a trained and canny speculator, a person who studies the public wants and supplies them at wholesale rates. The artist who studies the period styles of furniture for the manufacturer at Grand Rapids is not employing his time to preserve any artistic traditions. He is merely checking up on what will sell best in the market for the coming season. He is merely planning new models of old worn-out designs with one eye on the possible gross business and the other to avoid payment for original creative furniture designs. The stockholders of his company will point to the records at the end of the year to prove to each other which designs have been most artistic, on the theory that artistic achievement is measured only by a success computed in dollars and cents.

The discriminating public, however, is becoming more and more out of patience with the slick factory products. It is turning away from the highly varnished mahogany furniture, the factory-made cut glass and the other hundred soulless articles of merchandise. Take a walk through the average department store and you will see clearly how poverty-stricken the machine-made product appears and how this lack of originality and want of the individual touch give you a feeling of depression and fail to call up any sympathetic response. If this is the result of education and culture, if all this is the product of advancement and progress, then we must confess at once that here in regard to individuality in art and craftsmanship we have failed badly.

Once more let us return to the peasant family sitting peacefully before the fire during the long winter months. The big logs crackle on the open hearth. No one is allowed to remain idle. The women spin, card their wool and sew. The master of the house and his hired men are carving, mainly in wood, a great variety of household and farm objects of use. Huge collars for the horses in the field, as well as spoons and drinking mugs for the kitchen. And then there are objects of furniture to be added to the household and perhaps a cradle for a new arrival. But no one is allowed to sit idle. The designs are often very elaborate and very rich, but the feeling is always one of sincerity. While the colours of the finished product are often rich and gay, there is an earnestness behind the creation which comes forward.

It is in many cases difficult to draw a sharp line and indicate where the peasant art of one nation begins and another leaves off. Every province in Roumania has its own characteristic cross-stitch needlework, yet the entire Roumanian product blends in character with that produced by the peasant women in southern Russia. It takes a practiced eye to distinguish between the peasant craftsmanship of bordering countries, but one soon learns the difference between the arts of the different countries. The main characteristics of Swedish art are quite unlike the characteristics of the art of the Austrian peasant. But viewing any genuine peasant art one can imagine oneself back in the energetic days of the Middle Ages. The flavour of dense forests, the home of wild beasts, seems to spring forth from the purely geometrical designs in the best peasant creations.

It is hard to say where the peasant obtained the skill and knowledge that he applies to his decorative arts. Inevitably one feels that a certain amount of this talent was born with him and what he did not inherit he learned quickly from others about him.

The great grandmother in the family perhaps instructs the children in the type of needle work that she may have learned from an old nun three generations before. And in this way an accurate eye, a skillful hand and a clear peasant memory reproduce the art from one generation to another.

In recent years, a great vogue for peasant art has sprung up in most civilized countries. People living in industrial centres of civilization have discovered that there is a lesson to be learned from the serious and honest product of peasant workmanship. The lesson it teaches is that the machine-made product is, on the whole, a failure artistically and that at this price, art is hardly desirable. True enough, the price of the machine-made product is very low compared to the hand-made product, but artistically its value is almost nil. The artistic faculty is killed in most objects of machine creation, and the artisic faculties are aroused and inspired only by examples of workmanship that retain certain human characteristics and certain marks of individuality.

The work of the peasant may look small and ridiculous, it may seem primitive and crude and only a left-over from the old and passed-by civilization, but artistically it is a work that glows with pride and has the stamp and honour of serious workmanship. Just this little thing alone is enough to place it high above the conventional, punched-out, two-by-four machine-made product.

With the recognition of these virtues in peasant art, commercialism has again come forward and is now trying to take this art under its wing. This will result in no good. Already objects of peasant design are being manufactured in great quantities in order to supply this lucrative market. A certain amount of individuality is retained and the machine, like the wood-turning machine and the potter's wheel, is only used to help out and speed up the labour. Even in this regard the craftsmanship is losing its standards and the traditions are being swept away in order to supply attractive markets. When a great public becomes interested in any special field of art, it usually results in the degradation and degeneracy of that particular art. The arts in which the public is least interested have the best chance to retain their virtue.

What is the position of peasant art in relation to modern decoration? Is this note a desirable one in modern creation or is it again introducing a type of period merchandise, primitive in its character. To build a room resembling the interior of a primitive peasant hut in a fashionable New York apartment would seem most absurd. It would be just as much out of character with our surroundings and external life as a Louis XIV boudoir. As a rest from our age of extreme industrialism, as a diversion that will take us away from the machine age, a peasant character could with advantage be introduced into a small summer cottage used for rest and holiday. Peasant art seems to call for a natural background. It asks for green fields and trees and hills and in this setting, used sparingly, it offers a possible decorative advantage and escape from our busy age. The main lesson that we have to learn is individuality and character. These traits are stamped on every product designed by the peasant, and these traits are something we should try to preserve so that craftsmanship, pride of workmanship and the artistic traditions built up through the ages are not completely lost by this rapid push of modernism.

XII. INFLUENCES

AT all times varied outside influences have played important rôles on the stage of decoration. The past is never entirely wiped out in creating something for the future. Each period shows in its work not only the influences of its own time, but also traces of things that went before.

Modern art is modern, we said, if it presents a true record of our time. We insist that modern art is opposed to copying and is not greatly influenced by the periods that went before it. But this must not be construed to mean that all bridges have been burned behind us. A thorough knowledge of the historic styles that have played important rôles in their different periods, their peculiar characteristics, and their variations, are very important assets to workers in the field of modern decorative art. This knowledge is a guiding one and tells one what is best to avoid and what already has been done. It also gives one an idea of what the best artistic expressions of the past have been.

Modern art, in a way, may seem a very free expression of its time, one without rule, rhyme or reason. But this is hardly so. We find that examples of modern art, which are foremost in our esteem, conform to given rules and principles. These rules and principles are true of new art as well as of old art. Good art of all times presents certain dignified aspects of proportion and colour.

Influences from the past are before us daily, and not only these but influences of the present from foreign countries are also before us. Examples of the best modern art made abroad, as well as some of the ancient arts made abroad, lay claim for a part in the newly revived decorative arts in America.

Our chief influences in this country come from the work done in the art centres of Europe and the crafts of the Far East. American decorative arts have also been influenced by the important European, and latest American motion pictures, as well as by stage settings designed on both sides of the water. These various influences will form the topic of discussion in this chapter.

Long before modern European decorative arts could have influenced a movement in America to any appreciable degree, the Far East claimed our attention. It sent its art motifs across the world at a very early date, even long before America could be said to have been a civilized country. Every French château of two centuries ago displayed a series of rooms that formed what the French called a "Chinese Suite." These rooms were hardly Chinese, but they were a French interpretation of what they felt Chinese art must really be. These rooms contained a new kind of furniture which was an adaptation of Chinese raised lacquer work. The furniture was, of course, French of the period covered with lacquer work to give it a Chinese flavour. Lacquer work reached France at a very early date through the Dutch traders.

Not only did the Oriental influence touch the French château of two centuries ago but it also influenced Chippendale, master furniture designer. Some of his most important pieces of furniture he designed in the Chinese manner, and these distinctive creations we still call "Chinese Chippendale."

Each period finds its own interpretation and the special characteristics that it likes to reproduce. From the East we have had decorative objects made of bamboo, raised lacquer, inlaid mother of pearl, enameled metals, etc. Each period seems attracted to a certain type of work and these types have greatly influenced the decorative arts at various times.

Today we seek an escape from the over-decorated period rooms and try to gain that simplicity expressed in Japanese Shintoism of which the Tori, made of two upright logs supporting a beam, is the symbol. The two logs lean slightly toward each other and the crossing beam with protruding ends sags a bit and makes a subtle curve. The ends point heavenward and this form represents the gate in all the arts of the Far East.

The introduction of flat colours and plain surfaces can be traced back to the Japanese wood block and so also can a great many of our most modern colour combinations, such as black with red trimmings, red and yellow, yellow and green, and many others.

Many methods of decoration that have been used in the Far East for many generations are extremely modern with us. The extensive use of lacquers for furniture finishes, as well as for metals, the modern method of using gold and silver leaf in such a way that the different squares of leaf form an interesting pattern, the ideas of simplicity in ornament, as well as many others, are ancient practices in the Far East. In this connection, we must also mention the introduction of inlaid egg-shell as used in many of the decorations and modern lacquer works of Jean Dunand. And not only highly finished surfaces but the plain wood surface has also come to us through the master cabinet-makers of Japan. This influence has been very strong.

It would be interesting to compare the Oriental influences with those that we have received through the classical tradition. Should we go back into the history of art, we would find that all Western art was based on the classical ideal of beauty, as expressed in the Greek temple and crystallized in the Greek column. Our classical traditions brought us harmony in music, architecture and colour. It gave flowing movements to the dance, rhyme to verse, and it brought ornament into design. These harmonious characteristics of art are typical of the West.

On the other hand, Oriental art is not based on harmony but is built upon rhythm. The rhythmic relationship between the different parts is the secret that we learn from the Orient. This secret at once places the classical tradition in the background. The Venus de Milo, a statue of most harmonious forms and of classical proportions, which can be definitely measured, is no longer the standard of modern art. No such standards that can be measured by the size of the head exist in the Far East. Proportion is put aside for the sake of rhythm.

Rhythm has been the main influence from the East.

Of the various arts that have influenced American decoration the modern woodcut must take special mention. In this field, the Eastern interpretation is quite predominant. The vogue for Chinese prints has left an enduring impression upon the creative artist who turns to the woodcut as a means of expression. Tie-dyeing and Javanese batiking have also come to the front, as well as the gentle art of flower arranging, which, in Japan, is one of the most serious of all arts. It was not many years ago that our vases were looked upon as graveyards for our gardens. Large bouquets, while harmonious, were quite impersonal. The influence from Japan in the arrangement of flowers has resulted in our paying more attention to vases and flower holders. We are beginning to learn that different species of flowers require different types of holders. We are learning that there are characters and shades of meaning to different flowers, and we are also learning how to assemble them. The quiet simplicity that modern art strives to acquire is no better exemplified than in a single beautiful flower held in the proper holder and placed on a simple and dignified stand.

In speaking about the modern influences acquired from the East, it should not be understood to mean that complete Chinese or Japanese interiors are suggested for our Western rooms. Such a scheme would hardly suit the character of our country and certainly not the life. The influence of the Orient in our modern art is quite pronounced. It has left its mark much more strongly in America than it has in Europe.

The new modern decorative art movement in Europe began in 1897, in Vienna and in Darmstadt.

The artists' colony in Darmstadt, under Olbrich, and the Sezession, under Gustav Klimt, started the revolution in the world of decorative arts. Like all revolutions, the seed fell in many places on more or less fertile soil and the foliage that grew from this seed took on various aspects in the different countries.

The Austrian movement may be characterized as the "Byzantine Renaissance." The leaders of the modern movement in Austria have an enormous amount of decorative talent which expresses itself in colourful creations of all kinds. At first, the smaller objects used in the home took their attention, as well as poster art, book plates and book bindings, illustrations and book wrappers. The Austrian movement began with smaller things before it proceeded to the designing of furniture and furnishings on a large scale. Under the leadership of Joseph Hofmann, the Wiener Werkstaette for the last quarter of a century have held the field.

The main characteristics of this "Byzantine Renaissance" are that the objects are much bigger, playful, and often overdecorated, and, like a beautiful orchid that blooms best in a hot house, the art here flourishes in a decadent soil. It has never entered into the general lives of the people. It has never gained popularity. While the modern movement in Austria has not been very profitable for the artists and creative workers, the ideas originating there have claimed the attention of the entire world. Many of their creations have greatly influenced decorative art movements in other countries.

An attempt made a few years ago by Joseph Urban to open a branch of the Wiener Werkstaette in New York did not meet with very encouraging results, and the American public did not seem ready, or willing, to accept the Viennese school of art. The cool reception of the Wiener Werkstaette should not be used as an argument against modern art in general. If this exhibition had been temporary instead of permanent, it would have accomplished a notable result. However, Joseph Urban's initiative in bringing the work of the Wiener Werkstaette to America may be considered one of the initial stepping stones in the development of our modern art movement. It succeeded in bringing many new ideas, if only for a time, before the American public.

Next in the decorative art movement, we have to speak about Germany, where the development began simultaneously with Austria but proceeded along very different lines. The German character being entirely different from that of the Austrian, it, of course, had to express itself quite differently in the decorative arts. While the leaders in the Austrian movement showed an almost Oriental display of gold, silver, and ornamentation, the outstanding features of the German movement were mainly directed toward creations showing great restraint. The greatest merit of the work of Professor Peter Behrens, who is one of the leaders of the German movement, is its absolute freedom from any decoration. The main virtue of his designs consists in accentuating the necessary constructive features. This is true both in his buildings and in his interiors.

Looking back upon what has been accomplished in Germany during the past quarter of a century, the factory buildings erected by Professor Behrens for the Allgemeine Electrizitaets Gesellschaft near Berlin, are most expressive of their time and may be considered as the symbols of the present German movement. At the same time, the extremely simple interiors and furniture created by Professor Tessenow for the modern middle-class homes in Hellerau, belong to the best examples of modern art in Germany. The greatest contribution of Germany in the modern art field is along the lines of logical elimination and simplicity. It includes the introduction of new materials, which fit into modern schemes and take their places as parts of the main design. The Germans are thinkers and their art shows it. When they create with restraint, the result is often very good.

The objections that we have against many of the German examples of modern art are mainly directed against their clumsiness. This can easily be explained. The German Hausfrau will readily forego æsthetic elegance for the sake of usefulness and will insist that her bureau drawers are made extra deep so that they will hold as much linen as possible; or she will expect the dining-room sideboard to hold all the glass and china which we usually store in the butler's pantry. The gracefulness of a piece of furniture lies in its shallowness, and depth makes for massive clumsiness. There is still another reason why many German pieces are heavy, and that is because in Germany, most modern furniture is designed by an architect who plans it as he would a house. In most cases it is built to order for a special space and purpose.

For a long time France has rested on the glory of her past, and only after the war did she begin in a large way to pay any attention to the modern movement in decoration. In Austria and in Germany we find that the architects of these countries were the pioneers in the field, but in France the dressmakers were among the first to accept and to create actively in the modern manner. There are various reasons for this, one is that modern art and modern dress are very closely related; and another reason is that modern gowns show up to much better advantage against a modern background than they do against a setting of antiques. The dress designers needed new backgrounds.

The Exposition des Arts Décoratifs in 1925 was as great a shock to the average Frenchman as it was to all lovers of traditional art. A good deal of criticism from many quarters was directed against France because of this exhibition, but this undertaking can today be viewed in a more favourable light. The promoters of this exhibition showed very keen judgment for it was undertaken at a moment when it was still not too late to take up the banner and proclaim France the leader of the modern movement. Up to this time, France was far from being the leading nation in decorative arts and the exhibition, which was certainly a stroke of genius, marked a turning point. France is now again the leader of a new field—the field of contemporary decorative art.

The result of the international exhibition of 1925 in Paris was to bring the modern movement in France to the fore in a big way and it now embraces most of the leading industries and has the backing of the important shops. All the leading stores in Paris today have their own departments devoted to contemporary decorative arts and modern furniture. They are also employing the services of artists of repute to furnish them constantly with new designs and ideas. The smart shops of France are being decorated in the modern manner, and even the newest liner of the French Line, the *Ile de France,* is not only entirely carried out in the style of our time but in no detail shows any trace of imitating the traditional period styles. But it must be lamented that while there are many interesting features incorporated in this new French boat, it does not get very much closer to solving the problem that the modern ocean liner presents.

The French artist-decorator presents in himself a happy combination between the German architect and the Austrian decorative craftsman. The chief characteristics of his work are simple lines, graceful shapes, with a slight elegance, and a restraint in applied decoration. He is not hampered too much by the constructive features and many of his chairs do away with legs entirely and have bases that are made of cone- or cube-shaped forms. While the French modern expressions in decorative arts are certainly more acceptable to our taste than are the arts of other countries, we would certainly find it a heavy diet in the long run. The highly polished surfaces of modern French furniture, the use of exotic woods, ivory and carved handles, and extensive use of Japanese lacquer work, are all too sophisticated for our shores.

It would be interesting for a moment to look into the development of French fabrics and their design. Paul Poiret, famous for his revolutionary ideas in dress, was among the first to style and bring out an entirely new line of fabrics. These fabrics were designed under his supervision by the Martine School and show his genius as a colourist. Bianchini and Ferrier, the big silk manufacturers in Lyons, under the guidance of Raoul Dufy, are creators of a series of hand-blocked linens and damasks that must be admitted to be quite perfect. Raoul Dufy, who is one of the leading French artists, finds expression for his genius in block prints. Paul Rodier, on the other hand, expresses his talents in the art of weaving. In this art he is a great master. He was the first to give new expression to woolens for wearing apparel and now has extended his activities into the field of decorative fabrics. His designs are chiefly abstract, geometrical, and on a large scale. His stuffs are usually executed in one colour with shaded effects. He tries to find expression through the interest and attraction that comes from the weaving in his fabrics.

An interesting comparison could be made. While Poiret is creative through his bold use of colour, Dufy wants his wood blocks printed only in one colour and transfers the wood block idea, which emphasizes the design, to the cloth.

On the other hand, Rodier does not need any design at all and little or no colour, but makes use of shaded effects which he weaves into his cloth through the medium of the loom, and depends for his result very much on the finished texture.

We have now seen the various characteristics and trends of the decorative arts in France, Germany and Austria, and we have also spoken about the influence of the Far East. It is important that we should know what is being done elsewhere for, only by understanding the decorative world as it is at present and how some of the main features originated, can we hope to find our own place in the decorative arts movement. It is not possible to have these greatly intensified art movements in Europe without a certain amount of influence exerting itself on the creative American mind. But, while there may be sometimes a good reason for copying period art, there never is any excuse for the American creative mind to copy today's European art. The result would at once be evident and it would also be disastrous.

Will modern art live? And will this movement, which is now demanding so much attention, last, or is it just a passing flight of fancy?

The answer is: Yes, it will live!

And the reason for this is that the world has never gone backward but always on toward the future. If we are not satisfied with our art and artists of today it does not follow that we shall return to Queen Anne, but rather that we shall go on and develop along new lines.

Twenty-five years ago our automobiles were far from perfect, but it was soon realized that a good deal of our future depended upon the development of automotive power and never again were we to return to horses. Our airplanes are today in a position similar to that of the early motorcar. But there is no doubt in any one's mind that aeronautics has before it a great future. The new art development of today is also a child of the future.

William Morris died fighting against the machine age, but the machine survived.

Our progress of the future does not depend on fighting modernism but on educating ourselves to be part of the world we live in.

The seed is already planted and the ground—the soil of America—is fertile. Our duty is to keep the weeds away. Our duty is also to keep our minds young and not allow ourselves to be content with the accomplishments of the past. Every enterprise and each step of progress has been the outgrowth of vision. We today, in America, need leaders in the field of the decorative arts to show the same vision and the same spirit of pioneering which has made this country the most modern in the world. The world of today is the acorn of the world of tomorrow.

"La Miniatura," a residence in Pasadena, California, built in 1923 of textile-blocks, is typical of a new type of reinforced concrete construction. The square lines and terraced roofs, which have inspired recent European architecture, have for many years been typical of Frank Lloyd Wright's Prairie Architecture.

1

Architecture by Frank Lloyd Wright.

2

Founded in 1696, Trinity Church, an impressive Gothic monument in its day, is now hemmed in by the towering massive buildings of lower Broadway and Wall Street. Photographs by Ralph Steiner.

3

Two buildings with entirely too much architecture. At left the Woolworth Building, the highest and in conception, the most daring structure of its time, still faithfully adheres to Gothic ecclesiastical lines. The old Post Office at the right consists of rows of Classic columns and architecture placed one above the other.

4

A modern building and typical of the simplicity of today's architecture, though some of the motives have been inspired by the past. A system of vertical lines uninterrupted by an overhanging cornice are a feature of modern construction. Photographs by Ralph Steiner.

5

Between the old and the new. A solid block perforated by windows and capped with the old overhanging cornice. Repetition with very little rhythm or design. This shows clearly what the new step-back building laws have done for architecture.

6

Seen from the incoming steamer or the elevated railway, the Telephone Building is one of the most impressive additions to the lower New York skyline. The effect of this architecture, in which the massive towers build up and support the central block, is due to its not being lost in meaningless detail. Voorhees, Gmelin and Walker, Architects.

7

This picture of the French Building on upper Fifth Avenue shows the relation between the modern skyscraper and the ancient Egyptian Pyramid. The recessing of the upper floors gives an effect of high steps out of which the tower shoots skywards. Sharp contrasts of light and shadow accentuate the constructive beauty of the modern skyscraper. The architectural treatment of the adjoining building illustrates a comparison between the old and new ideas in skyscraper design. Photographs by Ralph Steiner. Fred F. French Co., Architects.

8

Architectural detail giving an idea of the scale used in ornamentation on skyscrapers. All decorative motives are geometrical as compared with the floral ornaments of ancient times. Buchman and Kahn, Architects.

9

Architectural detail of a modern building showing the vertical motive interrupted only by the terraces. Sharp angles give a great contrast between light and shadow. Buchman and Kahn, Architects. Photographs by Sigurd Fischer.

10

Like a spider web, this lacework of steel, expressive of our civilization, presents a beautiful pattern against a city sky. Photograph by Ralph Steiner.

11

A silhouette of Machinery. A picture painted in steel, expressive of our mechanical age and precision. Photograph by Ralph Steiner.

12

An old house effectively
modernized by Robert
Mallet-Stevens, Paris.

13

Private dwelling in Paris.
André Lurçat, Architect.

14

Two-storey concrete houses in the Hoek van Holland.   J. J. P. Oud, Architect.

15

Detail of the houses shown above.

16

Chilehaus, Hamburg, a modern structure, overwhelming in detail and too emphatic in decoration. An example of over-dramatized modernism. Fritz Hoger, Architect.

17

Typical detail of the Einstein Tower showing plastic architecture conceived and executed in reinforced concrete.   Potsdam.   Erich Mendelsohn, Architect.

18

The Einstein Tower, rising into the sky like a battleship from the sea, is expressive of plastic architecture and stands as a monument to the purpose it serves. Erich Mendelsohn, Architect.

19

The interior of the Einstein Tower, like the observation bridge of a boat, is simple and businesslike.

20

Combination desk and bookcase. The vertical lines and rectangular cabinets are interrupted by the half round table top. The same motive is repeated in the chair back. Executed in selected California redwood, trimmed with lacquered black. Designed by P. T. Frankl.

A tower bookcase of California redwood. The base band is made of rolled nickel-plated steel. Designed by P. T. Frankl.

The same simplicity and straight line typical of American city architecture marks this skyscraper bookcase. The exterior is black lacquer—the interior is finished in a contrasting shade of deep blue-green. The book compartments open on three sides and a space is fully utilized. Designed by P. T. Frankl.

23

Rising up against the wall like some building against the sky, this bookcase is finished in lacquer with contrasting trimming, and has a cabinet base. Designed by P. T. Frankl.

A modernistic nest of tables, executed in red and black lacquer, combines Eastern and contemporary American characteristics. Graceful unbroken lines, sharp angles and extreme usefulness are typical of this set. Designed by P. T. Frankl.

25

Lady's desk, fitting into corner, executed in rosewood, with zebra legs, ivory handles and ebony trimmings. Designed by P. T. Frankl.

26

Looking down on comfort.   Designed by P. T. Frankl.   Photograph by Ralph Steiner.

A composition in glass and silver. Large round mirror in silver leaf frame with Egyptian motive. The glass tables consist of heavy plate glass tied together by metal bands. Designed by P. T. Frankl.

Modern living-room from the exhibition of Abraham & Straus, Brooklyn. The mantel in various shades of gray has luminous columns of frosted glass on either side. Into the plain wall over the mantel is built a triangular niche lined with silver. The low mirror-top table in the foreground is executed in rosewood and ebony. Designed by P. T. Frankl.

Skyscraper dressing table. A full-length mirror, flanked with step-back cabinets on both sides, has a lacquer finish with silver trim and silver handles. Designed by P. T. Frankl.

Simplicity of line is the virtue of this craftsmanlike serving table executed in cherry. Designed by Ilonka Karasz. New York.

Small table desk and chair finished in two shades of lacquer with silver-plated handles and mirror top. Chair seat of snake-skin. Designed by P. T. Frankl.

32

Lady's whimsical desk built like a puzzle with drawers on four sides. The drawer fronts are silver leafed and each drawer has a different silver-plated handle. Designed by P. T. Frankl.

33

This cabinet is executed in china-red lacquer trimmed with black, and silver leaf. The spacious compartments are shelved. The mirror with a red frame is hung from heavy silk rope with long gray tassels. Designed by P. T. Frankl.

Sideboard of a modern dining-room done in white, crystal and silver. The flowers add the colour to this background. Designed by P. T. Frankl.

35

A large window softened by Chartreuse chiffon curtains serves as a background for a modern rendering of Oriental motives. Designed by P. T. Frankl.

36

Corner of a living-room. All fabrics by Paul Rodier. Furniture designed by P. T. Frankl.

37

Two stick-willow chairs designed by P. T. Frankl. The screen is painted on bath-towelling.

38

Secretary cabinet executed in a variety of exotic veneers, the figure in
silver inlay. Designed by Eugene Schoen, New York.

39

Dining room buffet, executed in a variety of exotic veneers, simple and massive. Designed by Eugene
Schoen, New York.

40

Living-room ensemble. Table desk of macassar, ebony and rosewood. Fireplace faced with hammered bronze bas-reliefs. Designed by Eugene Schoen, New York.

41

Hall wardrobe. Walls papered with silvered pattern and furniture in Chinese red and silver. Designed by Lucian Bernhard.

42

Corner of a young girl's bedroom. Walls and draperies light blue and ivory, dark brown carpet. Designed by Lucian Bernhard, New York.

43

This buffet obtains its modern effect by the selection of choice woods and contrasting grains. The handles of the side drawers are replaced by a fluted strip of moulding. Top is plated mirror and base black lacquered. Designed by P. T. Frankl.

44

Interior of restaurant Crillon, New York. Execution in white, gold and red. Designed by Winold Reiss.

45

French Study. Small writing desk combined with book-shelves, striking in simplicity and unusual in shape. Modern barrel chair at right is covered in plain material. The lighting fixture consists of a plain translucent glass cylinder, held in place by metal ends. Designed by Etienne Kohlmann. Executed by the Studium-Louvre.

46

Modern dining room on the French liner, *Ile de France*. The straw paneled walls in striking shades of red, blue and green as well as the brilliant coloured rug are typical of Paul Poiret's daring sense of colour. Executed by Martine.

47

Boudoir corner.   The semi-circular shape of the room has been used as a motive for the decorations and furnishings.   The table consists of two concentric discs, the chairs represent sectioned cylindrical forms and the sofa is designed along the same lines.   Designed by Louis Sognot.

Modern treatment of dining-room walls.   Rectangular alcoves accommodate buffet and side table.   New treatment of the plain mirror.   Designed by Marcel Guillemard.   Executed by Primavera.

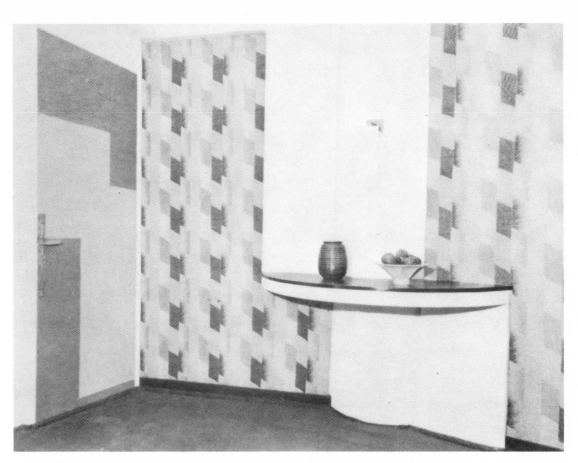

Section of dining-room showing Rodier materials for wall coverings and architectural treatment of built-in console. From the Salon des Artistes Decorateurs. Designed by Joubert et Petit. Executed by Dim.

50

Modern dining-room in distinct architectural treatment which strongly accentuates the horizontal line. Designed by Joubert et Petit. Executed by Dim.

51

Modern bar for the corner of a modern living-room in Paris. Walls are Parthenon pink, divan and bar stool are upholstered in pigskin. Designed by Djo-Bourgeois.

French dining-room. Walls are covered with decorative fabric of abstract design and shaded effects by Rodier. The plain surfaces of the side-board accentuate its soft curves. The wooden drawer handles introduce a vertical note in contrast to the horizontal tendency of this piece. Designed by Joubert et Petit. Executed by Dim.

Dining-room in a Southern French country house. The chairs and table are made of metal and the wall hangings are of striking geometric designs. In keeping with this are the simple lines of the furniture in which the constructive necessities are the only decorative elements. Furniture and fabrics by Djo-Bourgeois.

54

J. Dunand in Paris has revived the ancient Chinese art of lacquer work. The lacquered screens and furniture shown here are characteristic of his work applied to modern furnishings.

55

Modern smoking-room exhibited by Primavera at the Salon d'Automne. Metal chairs covered in maroon suède leather introduce a new note. Designed by Louis Sognot.

56

Modern bedroom furniture executed in varnished sycamore with bed cover in beige fur. Built-in book niches above bedside table. Designed by Kohlman. Executed by Studium du Louvre.

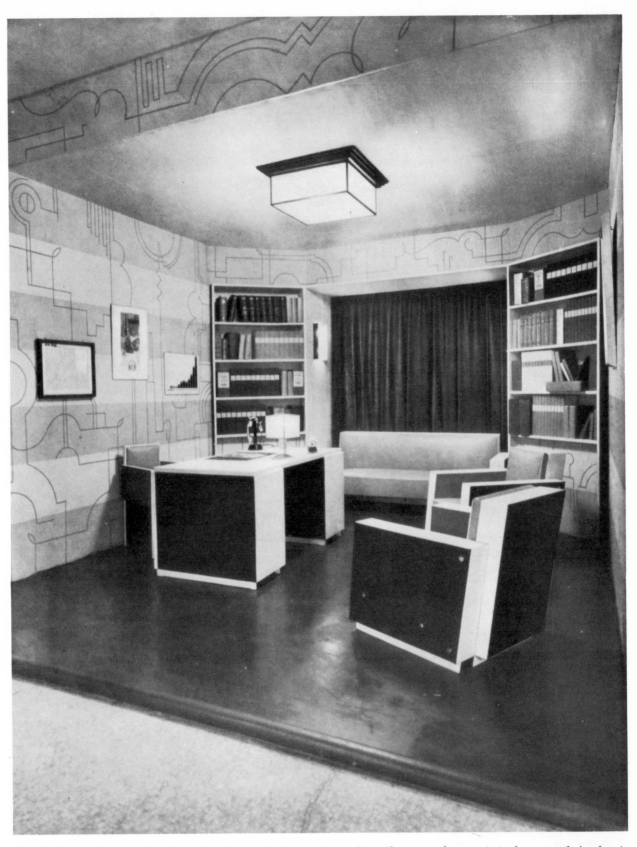

French Office. Extreme simplicity of surface with dominating cubist effects are characteristic features of the furniture in this room. The horizontal stripes along the walls are laced together by lines symbolizing mechanical and industrial drawings. The cube lighting fixtures of opaque glass harmonize with the setting. Designed by Georges Lamoussu. Executed by Lincrusta Walton.

Corner of a study, very architectural in treatment, with built-in recesses for books. Three disk table in black lacquer. Tubular lamp fixture in frosted glass lends a note of newness to the room though its practicability has yet to be proven. Designed by Adnet.

Modern mantel accentuating the vertical lines. The gilded mirror frame corresponds with the gold penciled design on gray wallpaper. Mantel by Marcel Guillemard. Sculpture group by E. Chassaing.

Dining-room side-board, extremely simple in line accentuating the natural beauty of the wood against a highly decorative frescoed background painted by Olesiewiez. Furniture designed by Marcel Guillemard. Executed by Primavera.

Private bar. The circular shape of the room is repeated in the lighting fixture, bar and stools. Designed by Louis Sognot. Executed by Primavera.

A picture in concrete.   Entrance hall in the home of the designer Raymond Nicholas.

Bathroom in green and blue mosaic — concealed light above mirror and faucets. Designed by Raymond Nicholas.

64

Another view of same bathroom. Shower and light fixture are combined. Designed by Raymond Nicholas.

65

A duplex bathroom with a triplex lighting fixture and a sunken tub. Designed by Gabriel Bouvier.

66

A step towards the glass house . . . all glass bathroom created by Lalique and exhibited at Salon d'Automne . . . oval tub in glass reinforced with silver strips . . . walls in narrow panels of glass.

67

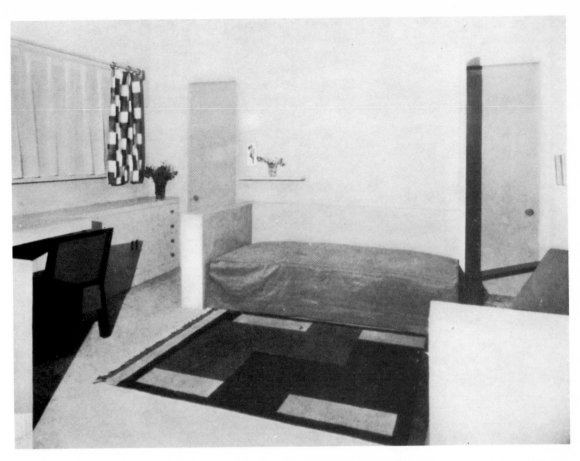

Striking simplicity and the long oblong motive as the only decorative element are typical for this room.
Designed by Djo-Bourgeois.

68

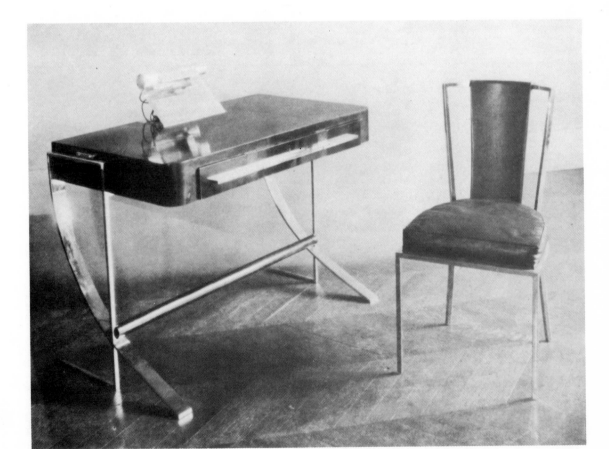

A modern desk with metal chassis in nickel plate and the top executed in walnut. The chair is upholstered with leather cushion and leather back. Designed by René Herbst.

69

70

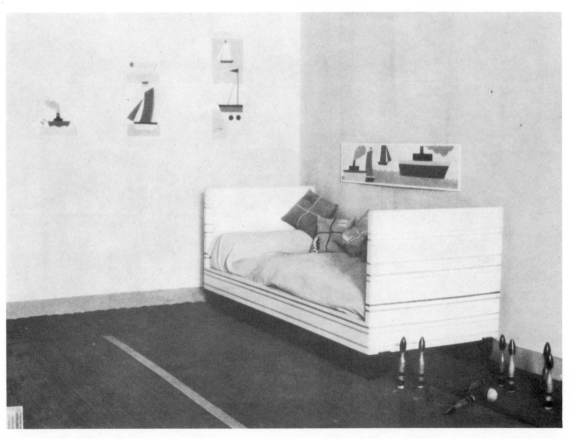

Corner of a child's bedroom with candy stripes on white lacquered bed. The pictures show simple renderings of boats to stimulate the child's imagination. Two of the walls are tinted moth yellow and the other two are pastel pink and chalk blue. Executed by Primavera, Paris.

A modern duplex conservatory with a spiral staircase giving movement to the room. The low furniture gives a strong contrast and makes the ceiling look higher. Designed by Marcel Guillemard.

Vestibulte, City Hall, Muehlheim.   The round arch, column and the sweep of the staircase are contrasted with the angular design of the ceiling.   Architect E. Fahrenkamp.

Swedish Hall from Paris Exhibition 1925. The extremely simple wall is broken by the elongated fire-place hood. A series of glass discs form the chandelier. Designed by Horvik.

74

Swedish living-room reminiscent of the Empire period. Architect, Carl Malmsten.

75

Porch in a German Country House designed by C. L. Klotz.

Study in modern German style reminiscent of the Empire period. Designed by Bruno Paul.

77

Upper hall in a German country house showing Chinese influence in the decorative scheme. Becker &
Kutzner, Architects.

Table and chairs designed by Paul Griesser.

79

Bedroom by Lucian Bernhard.

80

A German dining-room designed by Heinrich Tessenow.

81

Tea corner in living-room designed by Karl Bertsch.

82

Living-room corner in a country house designed by Karl Bertsch.

83

A simple alcove in a German home. Designed by Carl Malmsten.

84

Sideboard with interesting veneer and hardware. Designed by C. L. Klotz.

A simple buffet in pleasant proportions, interesting in its relation of surfaces. Designed by K. Bertsch.
Executed by the Deutsche Werkstätten.

Lady's secretary-desk. Designed by Fritz Reichl.

87

Dining-room buffet with interesting zig-zag veneer. Designed by Bruno Paul.

Simple secretary-desk and chair. Designed by Heinrich Tessenow.

Wardrobe with decorative painting by Joseph Hillerbrand.

90

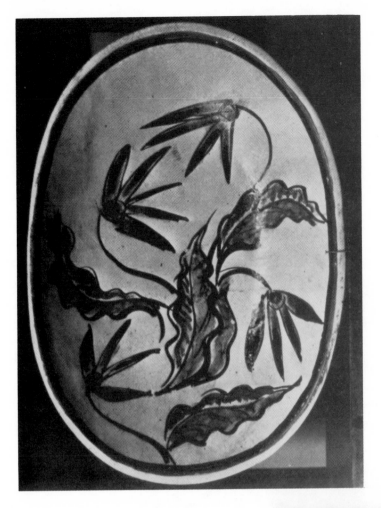

A large decorated plate by
H. Varnum Poor.

91

A large pottery jar by H.
Varnum Poor.

92

Dolphins in gilt bronze by Gaston Lachaise.

Terracotta tile for stove in relief sculpture, by Knut Anderson.

Detail of statue by Karl Trumpf.

95

Glazed terracotta in colours by Vally Wieselthier.

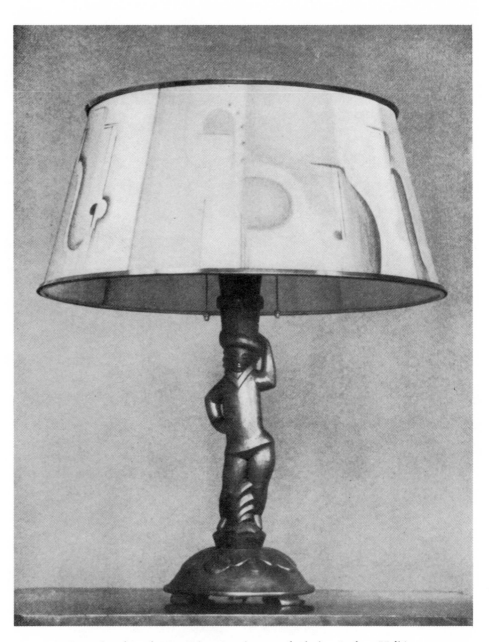

Carved walnut lamp with painted paper shade by Arthur Helbig.

97

Glazed terracotta by Max Läuger.

98

Fife and drum in porcelain by Mauritius Pfeiffer.

99

Geometric interpretation of the ceramics of today. Designed by Madeleine Sougez.

102

Two striking modern travel posters in blue and black on a white ground designed for the *Compagnie des Wagons Lits* by A. M. Cassandre.

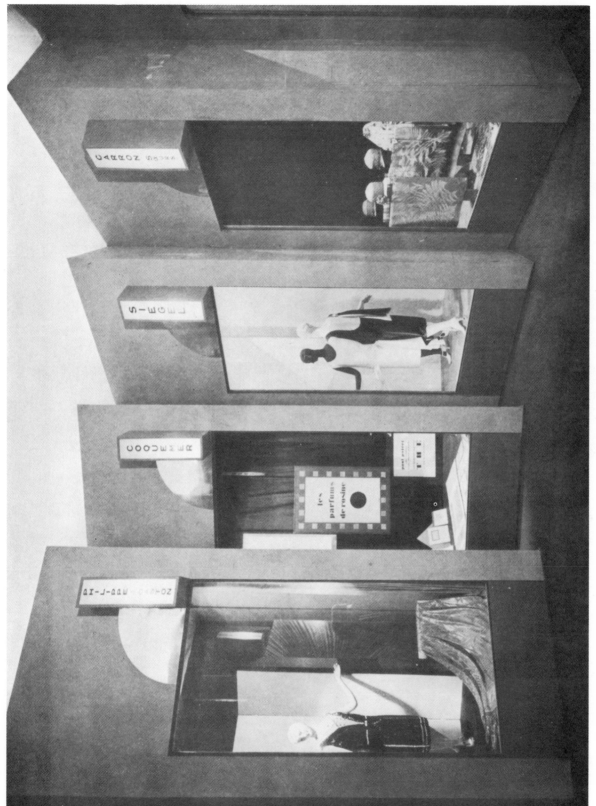

An amusing arrangement of a series of show windows. Designed by René Herbst. Executed by Siegel Studios.

103

Study in light and planes. . . . window display for *Siegel*'s stand at Salon d'Automne. . . . Façade in black and yellow, mannequin in light gray stucco. Light is thrown on figure from four different angles.

104

Modern window display for an hotel vestibule. Designed by Pierre Petit.

105

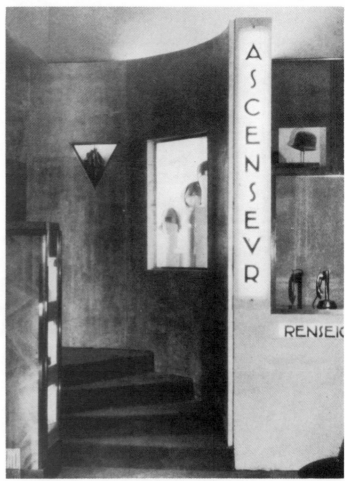

Exhibition pavilion of Cappellin's Venetian Glass, Salon d'Automne, showing the reverse effect of our modern step-back structures. While our buildings draw the eyes of the observer upward, this effect centres the attention on the most recessed inner part where the brilliant glass is attractively displayed. Designed by André Laroche-Garrus.

Two patterns of embroidered net for casement curtains executed by Paul Rodier, Paris. This design is purely abstract and geometrical in conception. The straight and semicircular lines of the embroidered pattern form a kind of grill and leave a decided background composed of small, dark, sharply pointed triangles.

107

The vertical lines seem to interlace and continue while the horizontal features of this shaded pattern are definitely broken and stopped. The wide horizontal zig-zag bands give rhythm and variety.

108

109

Two designs in metal work by Winold Reiss for the Alamac Hotel.

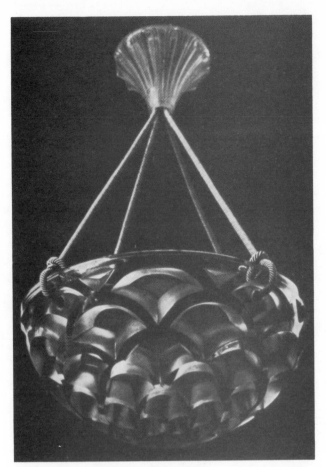

René Lalique sings his songs in glass. He has given new
beauty and expression to this medium. The lamp above
is executed by him.

111

Wall-paper design by N. Strauss-Likarz.

Modern mural decoration on a country house in Germany. Scene from the Bible in fresco decoration by Joseph Hillerbrand.

113

A striking note. Study in textures and shadows. Wood, felt
and glue form a pattern in this close-up of a piano mechanism.
Photograph by Anton Bruehl.

114

Dramatizing a typewriter.   A camera study by Ralph Steiner.

115

These designs have been painted with a camera. Matches and match boxes form one of the motives and simple lumps of sugar inspired the artist for the other design, both of which have been successfully executed in Stehli silks. The interplay of shadow gives an interesting pattern when photographed from above. Photograph by Edward Steichen.

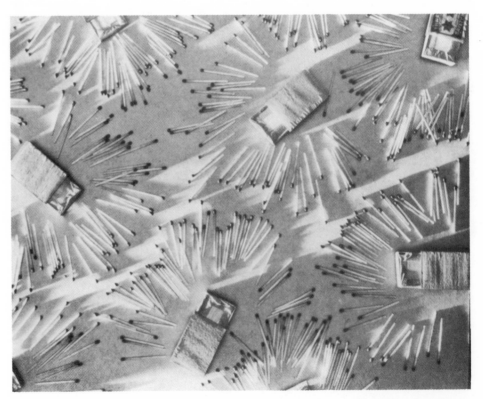

Macbeth.   The letter scene by Robert Edmond Jones.

118

Stage setting for *Back to Methusaleh* designed by Lee Simonson.

119

The "back-stage" of an Evangelist's Tabernacle for the play *Salvation*. Designed by Robert Edmond Jones.

120

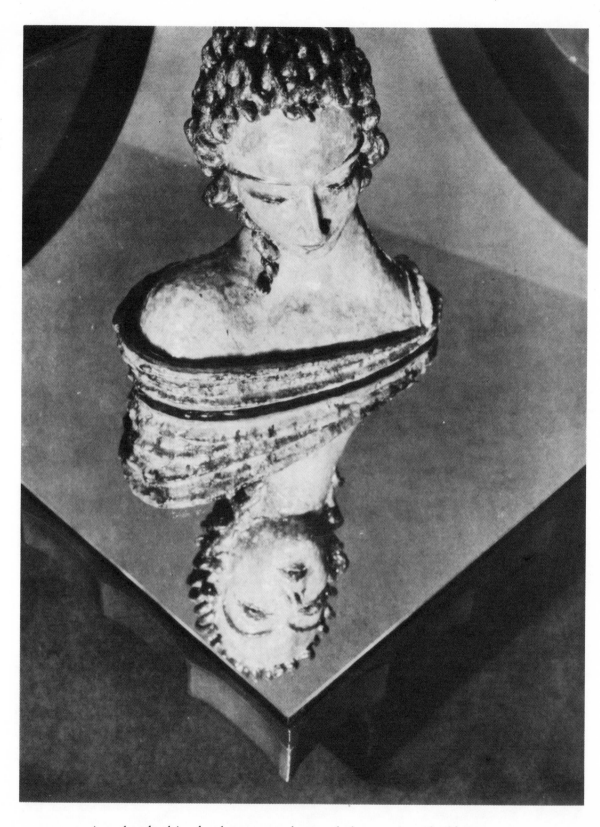

A modern head in glazed terracotta photographed on a mirrored table top.

Decorating is eliminating. This photograph is interesting not only as a study of light and shadows, but also in the architectural treatment of the wall. The narrow opening provides an attractive frame for the cactus and the decorative flower pot. The plain wall makes a suitable screen to receive the dramatic shadow. The cactus has established a very definite place for itself in modern art because of its simplicity of line, its interesting silhouette and relationship to modern form. Photograph by Ralph Steiner.